D0090890

I begged Shauna for this manuscript a year ago while it was half-baked. When I finally received it, I read it from cover to cover in one sitting, then sat down at my laptop and wrote four emails bowing out of engagements that no longer fit my life, made two hard phone calls, and gave an end date to two other commitments. *Present Over Perfect* loaned me the courage, integrity, and permission I'd been waiting for. I will go to the grave thankful for this message. It has changed my life.

—Jennifer Hatmaker, author of *For the Love* and 7

Most of the teachers I've had didn't think they were teaching me anything; they just thought we were friends. Shauna is that kind of friend, and this is that kind of book. As you turn these pages, you'll be reminded about what you have loved, where you've found your joy, and perhaps what you've misplaced along the way. Most of all, you'll be guided into an honest conversation about your faith and where you want to go with it.

—Bob Goff, author of *Love Does*

I cried tears of relief while inhaling *Present Over Perfect*. I cried because I'd completely forgotten that I don't have to earn worthiness, hustle for love, or fight to belong. Shauna's words—equal parts elegant and urgent—invited me to remember that my worthiness, belonging, and beloved-ness are birthrights. I can't think of a more important, more desperately needed invitation.

—Glennon Doyle Melton, author of *Love Warrior*
and the *New York Times* bestseller *Carry On, Warrior*,
founder of Momastery and Together Rising

I've watched Shauna walk this journey away from proving and pushing toward connection and grace, and as a friend, I'm proud of her. As a reader, I'm thankful to have these pages as an inspiration and guide. For all of us who yearn for meaningful, connected lives but find ourselves sometimes settling for busy, her words are the push we've been waiting for.

—Donald Miller, *New York Times* bestselling
author of *Scary Close* and *Blue Like Jazz*

Shauna awakens our desire to not miss our lives. Because that pursuit costs us our distracting habits, we need motivation beyond disciplines and rules. We have to want to really live and be with our people and enjoy this gift of a life that God has given us. Shauna's life makes me not want to miss mine, and her words here will make you not want to miss yours.

—**Jennie Allen,** founder and visionary of IF:Gathering, author of *Anything* and *Restless*

We live in a society that can easily have us running in circles if we aren't careful. And this can result in having a life full of things we actually never intended to sign up for. Shauna helps us take a step back and reset our minds and souls. In these pages you will find wisdom and encouragement to see past temporal success and accolades to experience the deeper, more connected and truly enjoyable life. After all, it is the power of connection with others that helps us thrive in every sense of the word.

—**Dr. Henry Cloud,** *New York Times* bestselling author of *Boundaries* and *The Power of the Other*

I have already read this book seven times. It's about pursuing the present over the perfect—but it is nonetheless a nearly perfect thing, a nearly perfect book. Shauna speaks exactly to my condition.

—**Lauren Winner,** author of *Girl Meets God*, *Still*, and *Wearing God*

With graceful confession, Shauna has created a memoir of her heart—a racing, fragmented heart that is becoming a contented, loved, and present heart. Reading this book heartened me for her, for her family, for her church, and for her generation. Shauna summons each of us to resist being sucked into the fast-paced draft of saying Yes and offers us a better way: the way of presence, the way of saying No. But this No is a Yes to something far better.

—**Scot McKnight,** author of *A Fellowship of Differents* and *The Blue Parakeet*

LEAVING BEHIND FRANTIC
FOR A SIMPLER, MORE SOULFUL
WAY OF LIVING

SHAUNA NIEQUIST

ZONDERVAN

Present Over Perfect

ISBN 978-0-310-34299-1 (hardcover)

ISBN 978-0-310-34671-5 (international trade paper edition)

ISBN 978-0-310-35176-4 (signature edition)

ISBN 978-0-310-34832-0 (audio)

ISBN 978-0-310-34304-2 (ebook)

Requests for information should be addressed to:
Zondervan, 3900 *Sparks Dr. SE, Grand Rapids, Michigan 49546*

Library of Congress Cataloging-in-Publication Data

Names: Niequist, Shauna, author.
Title: Present over perfect : leaving behind frantic for a simpler, more soulful way of living / Shauna Niequist.
Description: Grand Rapids : Zondervan, 2016.
Identifiers: LCCN 2016013557 | ISBN 9780310342991 (hardcover)
Subjects: LCSH: Simplicity--Religious aspects--Christianity.
Classification: LCC BV4647.S48 N54 2016 | DDC 248.4--dc23 LC record available at https://lccn.loc.gov/2016013557

Published in association with ChristopherFerebee.com, attorney and literary agent.

Cover design: Curt Diepenhorst
Cover photo: Aaron Niequist
Cover calligraphy: Lindsay Letters
Author photo: Sarah Carter
Interior design: Kait Lamphere

First printing June 2016 / Printed in the United States of America

For my boys

Aaron, I love how God made you passionate,
incredibly loving & fearless.
Henry, I love how God made you
wildly creative, brave & kind.
and Mac, I love how God made you exuberant,
affectionate & truly delightful.

Contents

Foreword by Brené Brown

A few months after I met Shauna for the first time at a speaking event, she emailed me to ask if we could get together during her upcoming trip to Houston.

Having recently finished her book, *Bread & Wine*, I was totally inspired to buck my normal response of "I'd love to, but I'm crazy busy right now" in favor of a hearty, "Yes! Come over and I'll cook dinner."

Shauna has a Benedictine passion about hospitality, gatherings, and feeding friends that I find contagious and inspiring. Of course, once the day arrived, my inspiration morphed into dread. My house was a disaster, I was two weeks late on a writing deadline, and I looked as tired and burnt out as I felt. What really sounded good was an evening of numbing out in front of the television with chips and queso. Alone.

In the middle of my "should I cancel or not" dance, I remembered this quote from St. Benedict: "Let all guests who arrive be received like Christ." Would I cancel on Jesus to hide out from my life with snack food and *Law & Order* reruns? Honestly, I hope not. But there are days when I'm not so sure. *And don't worry—God is totally clear about this struggle. We discuss it on a regular basis.*

On this particular day, I decided to welcome Shauna in the most holy way I knew—with love and total honesty. I heated up some turkey chili and tamales, threw on some comfy pants, and opened the front door. We hugged for a minute, then she looked me straight in the eye and asked, "How are you?"

I could tell she really wanted to know. I got teary eyed and said, "I'm tired. Confused. A little lonely. But holding on."

Shauna smiled as her eyes welled up. "Me too, pal. Me too. It's so hard sometimes."

Our time together that night was sacred for a simple reason: we chose to be present over pretending to be perfect.

I believe the most powerful way to share what it really means to show up and be present is through story, and that's Shauna's offering with this book. Her gift to us is a collection of stories that are real, honest, and familiar in a way that is both comforting and a little uncomfortable (like truth can be).

Present Over Perfect is an open-armed invitation to welcome the people we love, and even ourselves, back into our lives. It's not an easy call, but Shauna is at the door and she knows exactly how to make us feel at home.

God hasn't invited us into a disorderly, unkempt life but into something holy and beautiful— as beautiful on the inside as the outside.

1 Thessalonians 4:7, *The Message*

Wild Geese

By Mary Oliver

You do not have to be good.
You do not have to walk on your knees
for a hundred miles through the desert repenting.
You only have to let the soft animal of your body
love what it loves.
Tell me about despair, yours, and I will tell you mine.
Meanwhile the world goes on.
Meanwhile the sun and the clear pebbles of the rain
Are moving across the landscapes,
over the prairies and the deep trees,
the mountains and the rivers.
Meanwhile the wild geese, high in the clean blue air,
are heading home again.
Whoever you are, no matter how lonely,
the world offers itself to your imagination,
calls to you like the wild geese, harsh and exciting—
over and over announcing your place
in the family of things.

Ship to Wreck

And, ah, my love remind me, what was it that I said?
I can't help but pull the earth around me to make my bed
And, ah, my love remind me, what was it that I did?
Did I drink too much? Am I losing touch?
Did I build this ship to wreck?

—Florence + the Machine

This is a love story, like all my favorite stories. It's a story about letting yourself be loved, in all your imperfect, scarred, non-spectacular glory. And it's about the single most profound life change I've yet encountered.

One Saturday, three years ago, I stared at the ceiling of a hotel room in Dallas, exhausted. I said to myself, "If anyone else wants to live this life I've created for myself, they're more than welcome to try. But I'm done. I need a new way to live."

I was thirty-six years old. Aaron and I had been married for eleven years, and we had two boys—a one-year-old and a six-year-old. I was finishing a book—a month from submitting a manuscript, longer than the previous ones I'd written, and with recipes this time, which meant that during the weekdays I was writing essays, and in the evenings I tested recipes over and over, flinging pans of burned brownies into the sink and starting again, butterflying pork tenderloin, taking notes on paper spattered with vinegar, dusted with spices. On the weekends, often I was traveling, speaking at conferences, retreats, and churches.

In many ways, I loved this life—loved my husband, adored my kids, was so thankful to be a writer. But it's like I was pulling a little red wagon, and as I pulled it along, I filled it so full that I could hardly keep pulling. That red wagon was my life, and the weight of pulling it was destroying me. I was aware that I was missing the very things I so badly longed for: connection, meaning, peace. But there was something that kept driving me forward—a set of beliefs and instincts that kept me pushing, pushing, pushing even as I was longing to rest.

My health was suffering. I was frequently sick. I slept poorly and not enough. I got migraines and then vertigo. The muscles in my neck and shoulders felt more like rock than tissue, and the circles under my eyes looked like bruises. My heart—the heart I used to offer so freely, the heart I used to wear proudly on my sleeve—had retreated deep inside my chest, wounded and seeking protection. My ability to taste and connect and feel deeply had been badly compromised. My faith was stilted—it had become over time yet another way to try and fail, rather than a respite or healing relationship.

I loved my life, but I had become someone I didn't want to be around. I had become someone I didn't want to be.

This book is an account of my winding, messy journey from exhaustion to peace, from isolation to connection, from hustling and multitasking to sacred presence. And this book is an invitation, too—a hand reaching out across the pages, inviting you into that same journey, because it has been the greatest, most challenging, most rewarding sea-change of my adult life.

Not long after that Saturday afternoon realization, a mentor of mine invited me to an event with her in San Francisco, where she lives. I wanted to go. I didn't want to go. I didn't want to be away from my kids. I couldn't decide anymore what to do and what not to do, so I left her email in my inbox for a while, and then sent back a rambling, incoherent message about how my life felt so different than I thought it would, how I couldn't tell which end was up and couldn't put the brakes on, no matter how many times I tried.

She emailed back immediately. The line that stuck out to me was this: *"Stop. Right now. Remake your life from the inside out."*

For almost two decades, this wise woman's words have had a prophetic connection to my life—God has used her words in the right moments and seasons in such profound ways, and these latest words perhaps more than any others.

In that moment, I had no idea what it meant to remake my life from the inside out. Now, more than three years later, I'm so deeply thankful to look back and realize that's just what I've done, although in the twistiest, most circuitous possible way.

I tried all the outside ways first—I imagined the changes I needed to make were about time management, or perhaps having the cleaners come more often. I quickly found it was not about managing time or housekeeping. It was not about to-do lists or scheduling or minutes and hours. This journey has been about love, about worth, about God, about what it means to know him and be loved by him in a way that grounds and reorders everything.

I've been remaking my life from the inside out, and I want to invite you into that creative, challenging, life-altering work.

It *is* work, of course. It feels, I'd imagine, like adding a basement to a house that's already been standing for decades. I thought it would be more like adding new shutters, but I'm finding it to be more like lifting up a home and starting to dig, reorienting the very foundation. There is nothing superficial about this process.

Over the course of these last years, I've been to a counselor and a spiritual director and many doctors. I've prayed and fasted. I've read countless books. I've been on a silent retreat at a Jesuit retreat center, and another at a summer camp on Lake Geneva.

I've failed miserably and begun again, asked for help, asked for grace, asked for prayer. And beyond those things I've *done*, the more life-altering parts of the work are those things I've *not done*: the moments that I've allowed—or forced—myself to stop, to rest, to breathe, to connect. That's where life is, I'm finding. That's where grace is. That's where delight is.

I'm not, by any means, at the end of this journey. But I have traveled this beautiful new road far enough to know that this is how I want to live the rest of my days. I'm almost forty, feeling midlife-y like crazy, and this is how I want to live the second half of my life.

Richard Rohr says the skills that take you through the first half of your life are entirely unhelpful for the second half. To press the point a little bit: those skills I developed that supposedly served me well for the first half, as I inspect them a little more closely, didn't actually serve me at all. They made me responsible and capable and really, really tired. They made me productive and practical, and inch by inch, year by year, they moved me further and further from the warm, whimsical person I used to be . . . and I missed her.

The two sins at play here, I believe, are gluttony and pride—the desire to escape and the desire to prove, respectively. I want to taste and experience absolutely everything, and I want to be perceived as wildly competent. The opposite of gluttony is sobriety, in the widest sense, which is not my strong suit. And the opposite of pride, one might say, is vulnerability—essentially, saying *this is who I am . . .* not the sparkly image, not the smoke and mirrors, not the accomplishments or achievements. *This is me,* with all my limitations, with all my weaknesses.

It's as though God, in his graciousness and wisdom, pressed his thumbs into the twin wounds of my life, the desire to prove and the desire to escape, and in that pressing is the invitation.

What I'm learning, essentially, is to stand where I am, plain and sometimes tired. Unflashy, profoundly unspectacular. But present and connected and grounded deeply in the love of God, which is changing everything.

My prayer is that this book will be a thousand invitations, springing up from every page, calling you to leave behind the heavy weight of comparison, competition, and exhaustion, and to recraft a life marked by meaning, connection, and unconditional love.

Part 1

Sea-change

Full fathom five thy father lies,
Of his bones are coral made,
Those are pearls that were his eyes,
Nothing of him that doth fade,
But doth suffer a sea-change,
into something rich and strange,
Sea-nymphs hourly ring his knell,
Ding-dong.
Hark! now I hear them, ding-dong, bell.

—Shakespeare, *The Tempest*

Sea-change

Here I am, on the porch, and that feels fitting: outside as opposed to in, watching the water and the trees, listening to the music of the waves and the wind.

The word *sea-change* is from Shakespeare, from *The Tempest*: a man is thrown into the sea, and under the water he is transformed from what he was into something entirely new, something "rich and strange."

The beautiful and obvious connection, of course: baptism. We are tipped backward into the water, and raised into new life. We leave behind the old—the sin, the regret, the failings, and we rise out of the water cleansed, made new. A sea-change if there ever was one.

This is the story of my sea-change—the journey from one way of living to another. It's also an invitation to a sea-change of your own. No matter your age, your gender, your season of life, no matter your politics or profession, your sexuality or your faith tradition, you are invited into a sea-change.

I'm coming to believe that there are a handful of passages in our lives that transform us, not unlike conversions, where the old is gone and the new is come.

For me, this has taken the shape of a nearly four-year journey from exhaustion, multitasking, frantic and frayed living, into peace, connection, and rest.

When I look back on my life I can see a couple other sea-change seasons: One was my senior year of college, when I left behind chaos and disconnection for a renewed connection to God, to his people, to his Word and his ways of living.

Another was when I was twenty-nine and was fired from a job I held far too dearly. Also I was pregnant. And I was sitting on a book contract I was terrified to complete. That season was like off-roading, a little bit, like being plunged into new ways of living—writing, mothering, all the while grasping back to a job and identity that was no longer mine to grasp.

Years ago, a wise friend told me that no one ever changes until the pain level gets high enough. That seems entirely true. The inciting incident for life change is almost always heartbreak—something becomes broken beyond repair, too heavy to carry; in the words of the recovery movement, unmanageable.

In each of my three sea-changes, the life I'd created had broken to pieces in my hands. When I was twenty-one, my life was marked by drinking and dating and books, and only one of those things was helpful.

When I was twenty-nine, my attachment to my job was

such a white-knuckled thing, and I believe that getting fired was essentially God's grace prying my little fingers off that identity, digit by digit.

And in this current sea-change, my disconnectedness from my soul and from the people I care most about has become so painful that I'm willing to remake the whole of my life.

I've always been the bearer of what my husband calls "a Catholic imagination" as opposed to a Protestant one. I don't know where that came from, except that growing up in Chicago means growing up on all sides happily surrounded by Irish and Italian and Polish Catholics. We were the odd ones out, certainly, in our church that met in a movie theater, without crosses or priests.

More than that, though, I think this particularly Catholic imagination was born in me because my earliest loves—and my greatest loves to this day—were stories, meals, and water. Another way to look at it: the liturgy, communion, baptism.

I'm not at all an "in my head" person. I'm a blood and guts and body person, a dirt and berries and trees person. I'm a smell and taste and feel and grasp-between-my-fingers person, and both life around the table and life on the water are ways of living that I experience through the tactile sensations of them, not the ideas that float above them.

This sea-change in me began, fittingly, at the lake. I've spent summers all my life in this little lakeshore town. My grandparents had a cottage here, and both grandfathers had sailboats in this marina. My parents' first date was a walk on this pier. This town and this stretch of Lake Michigan is in my blood, deep in my bones.

For the last several years, each July, Aaron and the boys and I rent a house we love—a blue house with a wide porch and bright pink hydrangeas. We walk to the beach and the pier and the ice cream shop. We take the boat out every day, sometimes twice. We buy most of our produce at the farmer's market, and we pick blueberries and cherries to freeze and eat all year long. It's a three-hour drive to this small Michigan town from our house outside Chicago, but they feel worlds apart. I can feel myself exhale as we exit the highway and turn onto Phoenix Street, and the first glimpse of the water makes my heart leap every single time.

And so as is our custom, we arrived at the lake that July, breathless from travel, sleepless from kids, wrung out from a writing project that still wasn't finished.

Looking back, it's easy to see now that I was at my worst: weepy, snapping at everyone and everything, anxiety sky-high; deep connection to myself, to God, to the people I love most at an all-time deficit.

That July began the invitation to a new way of living, and each subsequent July has been a reset, a recalibration, a deeper invitation.

It's July once again, and I would never tell you that I'm

finished with this journey, all fixed up, nailing it. But I will tell you, with great gratitude and joy, that I am fundamentally changed, rebuilt from the inside. I have left behind some ways of living that I once believed were necessary and right that I now know were toxic and damaging—among them pushing, proving, over-working, ignoring my body and my spirit, trusting my ability to hustle more than God's ability to heal.

My life is marked now by quiet, connection, simplicity. It has taken every bit of more than three years to learn these things, and like any hard, good work, I fail and try again more often than I'd prefer. But there is a peace that defines my days, a settledness, a groundedness. I've been searching for this in a million places, all outside myself, and it astounds me to realize that the groundedness is within me, and that maybe it was there all along.

I've always trusted things outside myself, believing that my own voice couldn't be trusted, that my own preferences and desires would lead me astray, that it was far wiser and safer to listen to other people—other voices, the voices of the crowd. I believed it was better to measure my life by metrics out there, instead of values deeply held in my own soul and spirit.

And in the same way, I've always given my best energy to things outside myself, believing that I'd be fine, that I was a workhorse, that I didn't need special treatment or babying or, heaven help me, self-care. Self-care was for the fragile, the special, the dainty. I was a linebacker, a utility player, a worker bee. I ate on the run, slept in my clothes, worshiped at the altar of my to-do list, ignored the crying out of my body and soul like they were nothing more than the buzz of pesky mosquitoes.

Now I know that in the same way I've always believed God's Spirit dwells deeply in this world, it also dwells deeply in me. I've known that, cognitively, but my life spoke otherwise. Now I know that the best thing I can offer to this world is not my force or energy, but a well-tended spirit, a wise and brave soul.

My regrets: how many years I bruised people with my fragmented, anxious presence. How many moments of connection I missed—too busy, too tired, too frantic and strung out on the drug of efficiency.

Now I know there's another way.

You don't have to damage your body and your soul and the people you love most in order to get done what you think you have to get done.

You don't have to live like this.

Stuffed

Something reached fever pitch in my life, and then something snapped, died. And no amount of coaxing will bring that thing back to life again. Something, it seems, is over.

Maybe these things go in cycles. Someone told me recently that we experience a fundamental change every seven years. Maybe that's it. Maybe it's about having a new baby, one that we struggled for, one that arrived after a long and difficult pregnancy, one that will most likely be our last child, the baby of our little family. Maybe it's about biting off more than I can chew professionally—more books, more deadlines, more traveling and speaking. Maybe it's God, calling a big cosmic time-out on me, giving me a chance at a new way of living.

This is what I know: I've always been a *more is more* person, and something shifted this summer. Something inside me said *no more.*

No more pushing and rushing. No more cold pizza at midnight, no more flights, no more books, no more houseguests, no more of all these things, even things I love, things I long for, things that make me happy. No more. Only less. Less of everything. Less stress. Less crying. Less noise. Less TV. Less wine. Less online shopping. Less *one more thing one more thing one more thing*, whether that one more thing is a trip or a movie or a boat ride or a playdate. Less cramming 36—or 56 or 106—hours into a day that has only ever held 24.

One night with friends, we were talking about the future, about how to see what's next, how to know what change your life is leading you toward. One friend said that a way to get at your desire or dream is to answer this question: *if someone gave you a completely blank calendar and a bank account as full as you wanted, what would you do?* The first thing that leapt into my mind: stop. I would stop. I would rest. I would do nothing at all. I would sleep. The thought of it almost made me weep.

The important thing is not how much I did this year, how many trips I took—for fun or for work—or how much the baby did or didn't sleep (although *didn't* is the operative word). I want to tell you all those things. I want to make a case for why I'm so tired. I want to run you through the list, partially because I want you to feel it, to feel as tired and glazed and undone as I feel.

But also because I don't want you to think I'm weak. Not just any little thing could make me this tired. Not *just a baby* or something. Not just a book. I'm not one of those normal people who just gets tired sometimes. I'm so strong and full of energy. I'm so extra-capable and phenomenally tough.

I've been so committed to prove (as though anyone cares) that I can handle it all. And I've handled a whole lot of things. I've had babies and lost babies and written books and spoken at events and run races and hosted all manner of showers and dinners and parties. I've done so many things.

And I'm so tired. I miss my friends. I sleep terribly. I snap at my kids more than I want to, and then I lay in bed at night feeling guilty about it. I spend more time asking my husband for help with the dishes or the kids than I do asking him about his life and dreams and ideas.

Who wins, then? I handled it all! I showed them! But who is "them"? Who cares? Whose voice am I listening to? What am I trying to prove? What would happen, what would be lost, if I stopped, or if I slowed down to a pace that felt less like a high-speed chase all day, every day?

What if I trusted that there would be more time down the road, that if that book has to be read or that party has to be thrown or that race has to be run or that trip has to be taken, there will be time to take it/do it/read it/write it later? Later. Later.

I don't operate in *later*. I've always been proud of that. But look where it's gotten me. Stuffed. Exhausted. Wrung out and over-scheduled to the point where even things I love to do sound like obligations, and all my deepest desires and fantasies involve sleep and being left alone. My greatest dream is to be left alone? Things have gone terribly awry.

There has to be another way. And I'm going to find it. I'm going to make the space to taste my life once again. I'm going to find a new way of living that allows for rest, as much rest as I need, not just enough to get me through without tears, but enough to feel alive and whole, grounded and gracious. Things I haven't been in years.

What I ache for these days is space, silence, stillness. Sabbath. I want to clear away space and noise and things to do and things to manage. I want less of everything. Less stuff. Less rushing. Less proving and pushing. Less hustle. Less snapping at my kids so that they'll get themselves into the car faster so we can go buy more stuff that we're going to throw away. Less consumption. Less feeling like my mind is fragmented and my stomach is bloated and my life is out of control.

I feel like I'm driving a car 100 miles an hour with music blaring out of open windows. I screech into a parking lot, throw the car in park, sprint into 7-Eleven, and race to the back of the store. I throw my head back under the Slurpee machine, and I fill my mouth with red Slurpee, tons and tons, running down my face and neck. I just keep gulping and gulping, sticky red corn syrup-y sludge, more and more, until I stand up, smeared and dripping, and race back for the car, on to the next thing, jamming the car into reverse, music at mind-numbing volume.

That's how I feel. And what I want is one strawberry. In total silence. No 100 miles an hour, no music, no fake red mess all over my face and neck. I want one real strawberry. And I don't know how to get there from here. I am stuffed.

You can use whatever term you want: besetting sin,

shadow side, strength and weakness. The very thing that makes you *you*, that makes you great, that makes you different from everyone else is also the thing that, unchecked, will ruin you. For me, it's lust for life. It's energy, curiosity, hunger.

I'll come back around this block a thousand times in my lifetime, probably. I hope I'm getting better at it, hope that I'm righting the imbalance more incrementally these days than I was ten years ago. For the most part, I have been, I think.

But then the wheels fell off again, and I realized this time around, it's more than a tune-up, more than righting a pesky small imbalance. This time around it's about an overhaul, about digging around the foundations and the assumptions and building a new way of living from the ground up.

Because I'm stuffed.

Running Laps

I never know I need quiet and stillness until it's too late, till the lack of stillness scrapes me raw. Henry was sick this weekend, and then just as soon as he was on the upswing, Aaron got sick, and then Monday morning, when I so desperately needed everyone to be better, all three woke up sick—a boogery little boy, a big boy with a big barking cough, Aaron chilled and feverish.

And I was furious. Furious at whom, I don't know, because you can't help being sick. But what I felt was trapped and angry. I didn't want to wipe another nose, fold another little set of pajamas, measure out another dose of Tylenol. I wanted to leave.

Three sick boys, dependent on me, feels a little too much like the rest of life. I've spent a lifetime establishing my role as responsible party. What that means is that *I take care of it.* And by "it" I mean everything. I troubleshoot, multitask, strategize. Especially in seasons when I travel a lot, when I'm home, I'm in the zone—new pants for Henry, diapers for Mac, permission slips and orthodontist appointments.

If I'm honest, I overcompensate for my absences by trying to make my home time spectacular. Look, I didn't miss a beat! Look, you've got everything you need and then some! Look, you didn't even notice I was gone, what with all the perfectly folded clothes and perfectly washed grapes and perfectly planned activities. I hate being gone, so I make sure that when I'm home, I'm super-home, lots of homemade meals and clean closets, as emphatically *home* as possible.

And so, on that first morning that Henry was sick, I was cleaning up from the party we'd had the night before—ten adults and ten kids. I was unpacking our bags from our trip to South Haven the day before that. I was laundering new bedding for Henry's room and stuffing a duvet into its new case, puttering around, putting things away.

This is what I call fake-resting. I'm wearing pajamas. The kids are watching cartoons, snuggling under blankets, eating waffles. Aaron's reading or sleeping. It looks like I'm resting, too. But I'm not. I'm ticking down an endless list, sometimes written, always mental, getting things back into their right spots, changing the laundry, wiping down the countertops.

Some might say this is being a mother, or a homemaker, or this is what women have been doing for generations: tending to the home stuff while men and children go about their leisure. Maybe so, but this woman and mom is exhausted. And tired of being exhausted.

So I fake-rested on Saturday, and then again on Sunday.

The kids and Aaron napped. They played with Legos and went to bed early. They watched movies and ate leftover pumpkin pie. And I caught up on emails and ordered Christmas presents and cleaned out a closet and started packing for an upcoming trip.

I fake-rested instead of real-rested, and then I found that I was real-tired. It feels ludicrous to be a grown woman, a mother, still learning how to rest. But here I am, baby-stepping to learn something kids know intuitively.

Part of being an adult is taking responsibility for resting your body and your soul. And part of being an adult is learning to meet your own needs, because when it comes down to it, with a few exceptions, no one else is going to do it for you.

Frankly, the men I know don't generally struggle with this. They've been raised to eat when they're hungry, sleep when they're tired, run when they're antsy, leave when they're ready to leave. But even the most driven, articulate, strong women I know struggle to really meet their own needs.

A friend and I recently talked about how deeply invested we both are in people thinking that we're low maintenance—we both want to be seen as flexible, tough, roll-with-anything kinds of women. And this ends up keeping us from asking for what we need, for fear of being labeled difficult or diva-ish. But what good is it doing me to have people think I'm laid-back and flexible . . . when really that cherished reputation keeps me tangled up, needs unmet, voice silenced?

I knew that I needed to work less. That's absolutely true. That's the first step. But it's trickier than that: the internal voice that tells me to hustle can find a to-do list in my living room as easily as it can in an office. It's not about paid employment. It's about trusting that the hustle will never make you feel the way you want to feel. In that way, it's a drug, and I fall for the initial rush every time: if I push enough, I will feel whole. I will feel proud, I will feel happy. What I feel, though, is exhausted and resentful, but with well-organized closets.

Who told me that keeping everything organized would deliver happiness? What a weird prescription for happiness. Why do I think managing our possessions is a meaningful way of spending my time? Why do I think clean countertops means anything at all? Well, certainly, my Dutch roots might have something to do with it, and my Midwestern upbringing.

And I know that activity—any activity—keeps me from feeling, so that becomes a drug, too. I'll run circles around this house, folding clothes and closing cabinets, sweeping and tending to things, never allowing myself to feel the cavernous ache.

Which brings us, literally, to the heart of the conversation: the heart, the cavernous ache. Am I loved? Does someone see me? Do I matter? Am I safe?

For most of my life, I've answered these questions with theological abstractions, and then filled up any remaining uncertainty with noise and motion and experiences. In my teens and early twenties, this was mostly road trips and closing down bars and kissing and all manner of adventures. And then somewhere along the way that frantic energy translated itself into work, that same manic devotion to keeping things moving, but this time not on the dance floor.

I learned a long time ago that if I hustle fast enough, the emptiness will never catch up with me. First I outran it by traveling and dancing and drinking two-for-one whiskey sours at Calypso on State Street in Santa Barbara. Then I outran it by lining up writing deadlines like train tracks and clicking over them one by one. Then I outran it by running laps around my living room, picking up toys and folding blankets, as recently as yesterday.

You can make a drug—a way to anesthetize yourself—out of anything: working out, binge-watching TV, working, having sex, shopping, volunteering, cleaning, dieting. Any of those things can keep you from feeling pain for a while—that's what drugs do. And, used like a drug, over time, shopping or TV or work or whatever will make you less and less able to connect to the things that matter, like your own heart and the people you love. That's another thing drugs do: they isolate you.

Most of us have a handful of these drugs, and it's terrifying to think of living without them. It *is* terrifying: wildly unprotected, vulnerable, staring our wounds right in the face. But this is where we grow, where we learn, where our lives actually begin to change.

Dethroning the Idol

Busyness is an illness of the spirit.

—Eugene Peterson

I come from a long line of hard workers—sheet metal workers, farmers, people for whom work is an estimable thing, something to respect and be grateful for. I got my first summer job when I was eleven. I rode my bike two miles to the windsurfer shop down by the marina in South Haven, and while the owner and his friends—all in their twenties—slept off hangovers and ran out to the beach at a moment's notice if the wind piped up, I decorated the shop's window displays and rearranged the stickers and sunglasses.

And I went to one of those high schools where much was expected of us—AP classes and academic scholarships to good colleges, high test scores, loads of extracurriculars rounding out our applications. While I was in high school, I was also volunteering several days a week and a few nights at my church, too—devoted to the high school ministry, teaching Sunday school to grade school kids. And I worked at the Gap, and at Boloney's, a much-loved deli near my high school.

In college, I was all over the map spiritually and couldn't be bothered to attend chapel or church, but I took a full class load every semester, worked in the library, and worked at a summer camp that kept me running from morning till night, quite literally.

All that to say, I've been working all my life. Work has been a through line, one that I'm very thankful for, one that has taught me so much about the benefits of structure, discipline, skill, communication, and responsibility.

But at some point, good clean work became something else: an impossible standard to meet, a frantic way of living, a practice of ignoring my body and my spirit in order to prove myself as the hardest of hard workers.

As I unravel the many things that brought me to this crisis point, one is undeniably my own belief that hard work can solve anything, that pushing through is always the right thing, that rest and slowness are for weak people, not for high-capacity people like me.

Oh, the things I did to my body and my spirit in order to maintain my reputation as a high-capacity person. Oh, the moments I missed with people I love because I was so very committed to being known as the strongest of the strong. Oh, the quiet moments alone with God I sacrificed in order to cross a few things off the to-do list I worshiped.

Productivity became my idol, the thing I loved and valued

above all else. We all have these complicated tangles of belief and identity and narrative, and one of the early stories I told about myself is that my ability to get-it-done is what kept me around. I wasn't beautiful. I didn't have a special or delicate skill. But I could get stuff done, and it seemed to me that ability was my entrance into the rooms into which I wanted to be invited.

I couldn't imagine a world of unconditional love or grace, where people simply enter into rooms because the door is open to everyone. The world that made sense to me was a world of earning and proving, and I was gutting it out just like everyone around me, frantically trying to prove my worth.

Over time, a couple things happened. I wish I could tell you that when my health suffered, I paid attention, listened to my body, changed course. I did not. I kept going when I was sick, when I was pregnant, when I was still bleeding from a miscarriage. I kept going when I had vertigo—seasick on dry land—when I couldn't sleep past 3 a.m., when I threw up a couple times a week in stressful situations.

But what I eventually realized is that the return on investment was not what I'd imagined, and that the expectations were only greater and greater. When you devote yourself to being known as the most responsible person anyone knows, more and more people call on you to be that highly responsible person. That's how it works. So the armload of things I was carrying became higher and higher, heavier and heavier, more and more precarious.

At the same time, I was more and more aware that I was

miserable. Not all the time, of course, but sometimes, in those rare moments when I let myself really feel honestly instead of filling in the right answers, I realized with great surprise that this way of living was not making me happy at all.

People called me tough. And capable. And they said I was someone they could count on. Those are all nice things. Kind of. But they're not the same as loving, or kind, or joyful. I was not those things.

I believed that work would save me, make me happy, solve my problems; that if I absolutely wore myself out, happiness would be waiting for me on the other side of all that work. But it wasn't.

On the other side was just more work. More expectations, more responsibility. I'd trained a whole group of people to know that I would never say no, I would never say "this is too much." I would never ask for more time or space, I would never bow out. And so they kept asking, and I was everyone's responsible girl.

And I was so depleted I couldn't even remember what whole felt like. I felt used up by the work, but of course it was I who was using the work, not the other way around. I was using it to avoid something, to evade something. I was using it to prevent myself from becoming acquainted with the self who sat hidden by all the accomplishment. I wanted to get to know that person, make friends with her. I wanted to learn to beckon her out from behind the accomplishment, and, when the wind piped up, take her off to the sea.

You Put Up the Chairs

I hope you live a life you're proud of. If you find that you are not, I hope you have the strength to start all over again.

—F. Scott Fitzgerald

I was at a pool party with some of my oldest, most-favorite friends. I've known them since high school, so at this point they feel more like sisters. Anyone who knew you as an adolescent and still wants to spend time with you is a true friend, and really, their opportunity to blackmail you with stories of who you kissed and photos of you in overalls is enough reason to keep them around. We don't see each other nearly often enough, but when we do, we fall right back into familiar rhythm, like a song we've been singing all our lives.

While we watched our kids jump off the diving board and dive for rings, while Jenny's husband grilled chicken and we drank lemonade icy from the cooler, we had the same conversation we always have when we see each other: we should get together more. *It's just so busy, everyone's so busy. Kids, you know. School, right? Work is insane. Piano and hockey. In-laws and baby showers and moving houses and book club and who has time?*

And then someone buttoned up that conversation the same way we always do: *But what are you going to do?*

We murmured agreement, sipped our lemonade, dangled our legs in the cool water, reminded our kids not to run near the pool.

And on the way home, I couldn't help but think about that conversation, and in particular, that phrase: *But what are you going to do?*

There we were, women in our thirties. Educated, married, mothers, women who have careers, who manage homes and oversee companies. And there we were, utterly resigned to lives that feel overly busy and pressurized, disconnected and exhausted.

But that's shifting the blame, right? Who's the boss, if not us? Who's forcing us to live this way? Or, possibly, do we *not* want to face the answer to that question, preferring to believe we can't possibly be held responsible for what we've done?

Years ago, Aaron and I were talking with the pastor of a fast-growing church, and another friend, a more seasoned pastor. The first pastor was telling the story of how the church had exploded, how they couldn't stop the growth, how it was utterly out of their control, an inexplicable, unstoppable phenomenon.

The seasoned pastor pushed him gently: "You've built

this, and it's okay to say that. You've intentionally and strategically built a very large church. It's okay to say that."

The young pastor kept protesting, preferring the narrative of wild and unexplained growth. "We had nothing to do with it," he insisted.

"Well, not nothing," said the older pastor. "You kept putting up more chairs."

And then our minds sort of exploded, because it didn't occur to us that there was another option. We were all raised to build, build, build. Bigger is better, more is better, faster is better. It had never occurred to us, in church-building or any other part of life, that someone would intentionally keep something small, or deliberately do something slow.

This conversation happened more than a decade ago, before slow food and artisanal everything, before a cultural return to handmade and homemade, toward limited editions and small-batch cooking.

And even though small-batch cooking is now all the rage, for those of us who came of age in the "more is more" mentality, it can be hard to grasp the idea that we have some say over the size of our own lives—that we have the agency and authority and freedom to make them smaller or larger, heavier or lighter.

We were playing Legos a few weeks ago, and Aaron and I asked Henry about what he wants for our family in the next year. More adventures? More trips? Does he want to play soccer again? Does he want to start piano, or move to a different town, or get bunk beds?

"More this," he said. "More time all together like this.

And at home. I like it when we're all together at home." Aaron and I looked at one another over his head, letting the other know that we heard it, too, that we were paying attention.

Aaron and I are both intense, passionate people. We're artists and makers, and neither of us ever saw ourselves in a leave-work-at-the-office, nine-to-five kind of arrangement. When we were single, we worked around the clock, and loved it. And when we were married without kids, we did the same—we worked together, yelling across the hall from one office to the other about where we should stop for dinner on the way home, often after 10 p.m.

But now those patterns are being upended, for our two wild and silly darlings. And although we're making the changes for them, I can see how the changes benefit our neighbors and extended families and church community. And I can see very clearly how these changes benefit our marriage.

Loving one's work is a gift. And loving one's work makes it really easy to neglect other parts of life.

Aaron and I are talking a lot these days about work and time and calling, hoping to hold each one of them in their appropriate place, hoping to be honest about which ones matter more than the others.

Being good at something feels great. Playing ninja turtles with two little boys for hours on end is sometimes less great. It's so easy to hop on a plane or say yes to one more meeting or project, to get that little buzz of being good at something, or the pleasure bump of making someone happy, or whatever it is that drives you.

And many of us continue to pretend we don't have a choice—the success just happened, and we're along for the ride. The opportunities kept coming, and anyone in our position would have jumped to meet them.

But we're the ones who keep putting up the chairs.

If I work in such a way that I don't have enough energy to give to my marriage, I need to take down some chairs. If I say yes to so many work things that my kids only get to see tired mommy, I need to take down some chairs.

I know I've let my work win sometimes. I know I've gotten the math wrong, sometimes unwittingly, believing I could fit in more than I could. There have been times I've hidden behind my work, because work is easier to control than a hard conversation with someone you love.

That's part of the challenge of stewarding a calling, for all of us: you get it wrong sometimes. And part of stewarding that calling is sometimes taking down some chairs. We have more authority, and therefore, more responsibility than we think. *We* decide where the time goes. There's so much freedom in that, and so much responsibility.

That old question: *But what are you going to do?*

I'm going to take down some chairs.

The Word That Changed Everything

The word that changed everything, of course, is *no*. I'd been saying *yes* and *yes* and *yes*, indiscriminately, haphazardly, resentfully for years. And I realized all at once that I'd spent all my *yeses*, and in order to find peace and health in my life, I needed to learn to say *no*.

People love it when you say *yes*, and they get used to it—they start to figure out who the people are who will always say *yes*, always come through, always make it happen.

If you are one of these people, it does cause a little freak-out when you begin saying *no*. People are not generally down with this right away. That's okay.

You may know that *yes* is an important word for me. Maybe you've seen my *yes* sweatshirt, my *yes* earrings, my *yes* tote bag, my *yes* tattoo. I'm not kidding about any of those things. *Yes* matters to me on a deep level—saying a broad and brave *yes* to this beautiful world, to love and challenge and hard laughter and dancing and trying and failing. *Yes* is totally my jam.

But you can't have *yes* without *no*. Another way to say it: if you're not careful with your *yeses*, you start to say *no* to some very important things without even realizing it. In my rampant *yes-yes-yes*-ing, I said *no*, without intending to, to rest, to peace, to groundedness, to listening, to deep and slow connection, built over years instead of moments.

All my *yeses* brought me to a shallow way of living—an exhausting, frantic lifestyle that actually ended up having little resemblance to that deep, brave *yes* I was searching for.

And so if you, like me, have said too many *yeses*, and found that all that hopeful, exciting, wide-open intention has actually left you scraped raw and empty, the word that can change everything is *no*.

I know. I don't like it either. *Yes* is fun and sparkly and printed on tote bags. *No?* What if you saw someone wearing a sweatshirt that just said *no*? I do not want to sit next to that bundle of fun.

But *no* became the scalpel I wielded as I remade my life, slicing through the tender tissue of what needed to go and what I wanted to remain.

My mentor's words rang in my ears: *Stop. Right now. Remake your life from the inside out.* I don't know a way to remake anything without first taking down the existing structures, and that's what *no* does—it puts the brakes on your screaming-fast life and gives you a chance to stop and inspect just exactly what you've created for yourself, as difficult as that might be.

It was very difficult for me to learn to say no. I did it badly, awkwardly, sometimes too forcefully, and sometimes with so many disclaimers and weird ancillary statements that people actually had no idea what I was saying. I hovered endlessly after I said it—*Was that okay? Are we okay? Because I love you—you know I love you, right? We're okay?*

But like anything you learn, it gets easier over time. You begin to build up muscle memory for what it feels like to say exactly what you feel, what you need, what your limitations are. And a very interesting thing begins to happen: some people peer into your face with fascination—*I want some of that,* essentially, is what they're saying. Your honesty and freedom is giving them the permission to be honest and free as well.

And some people are not down with this way of living at all. They'd prefer you continue over-functioning for their own purposes, thank you very much. Or they're so wrapped up in their own hyper-functioning life that it's a personal affront to their value system when you say something insane like, "I'm sorry, I can't do that."

Bless them. But don't spend too much time with them. Draw close to people who honor your *no*, who cheer you on for telling the truth, who value your growth more than they value their own needs getting met or their own pathologies celebrated.

Our little Cooking Club—my day-to-day lifeline best people—we're cheering each other on along this journey, and it makes all the difference. We talk every day, usually many times a day, and our constant refrain sounds like this: what can you lay down? How can we make this simpler? Are you getting enough rest? Can I take your kids for a couple hours?

Instead of competing for who's busier or who's more tired, who's keeping more balls in the air, we're constantly looking for ways to help each other's lives get lighter, easier to carry, closer to the heart of what we love, less clogged with expectations and unnecessary tasks. These women are like my training wheels as I learn this, keeping me upright as I wobble along, and I'm so thankful.

And don't worry: *no* won't always be the word you use most often. I hate that for a season, *no* had to be the answer to almost everything. But over time, when you rebuild a life that's the right size and dimension and weight, full of the things you're called to, emptied of the rest, then you do get to live some *yes* again. But for a while, *no* is what gets you there.

On Disappointing People

Some people are very uncomfortable with the idea of disappointing anyone. They think that if you are kind, you'll never disappoint anyone. They think that if you try hard enough, if you manage your time well enough, if you're selfless enough, prayerful enough, godly enough, you'll never disappoint anyone. I fear these people are headed for a rude awakening.

I know this, because I was one of those people. For so many years, I was deeply invested in people knowing that I was a very competent, capable, responsible person. I needed them to know that about me, because if that was true about me, I believed, I would be safe and happy. If I was responsible and hardworking, I would be safe and happy.

Fast forward to a deeply exhausted and resentful woman, disconnected from her best friends, trying so darned hard to keep being responsible, but all at once, unable. Something snapped, and my anger outweighed my precious competence. Something fundamental had to change.

This is what I know for sure: along the way you will disappoint someone. You will not meet someone's needs or expectations. You will not be able to fulfill their request. You will leave something undone or poorly done. Possibly, this person will be angry with you, or sad. You've left them holding the bag. Or maybe instead of sadness or anger, they'll belittle you or push all your shame buttons—maybe they'll say things like, "I guess you're just not a hard worker." Or, "I guess you're just a low-capacity person." Or, "I thought I could count on you." These are basically sharp blades straight into the hearts of people like me, people who depend very heavily on meeting people's expectations.

But here's the good news: you get to decide who you're going to disappoint, who you're going to say *no* to. And it gets easier over time, the disappointing.

What you need along the way: a sense of God's deep, unconditional love, and a strong sense of your own purpose. Without those two, you'll need from people what is only God's to give, and you'll give up on your larger purpose in order to fulfill smaller purposes or other people's purposes.

To be sure, finding your purpose can take a long time to figure out, and along the way it is tempting to opt instead for the immediate gratification, the immediate fix, of someone's approval. But the sweet rush of approval, the pat on the head, can often derail us from real love, and real purpose.

Time always helps me make these decisions, because if I'm rushed, I always say yes. When I have time, I can instead say to myself: *Go back to being loved; go back to your purpose.*

This thing I am being asked to do will not get me more love. And this will not help me meet my purpose.

Some of us have trouble disappointing people in authority. Or people we want to impress, or people who seem fancy or important in some way. I've realized one thing that makes it hard for me to disappoint people is my tendency to overestimate how close I am to someone, and then how imperative it is that I don't disappoint this dear, dear friend. But upon closer inspection, I am probably not this person's dear friend. This is probably not a deep heart wound, but probably more a small professional disappointment. Those are very different. And there's a difference between forsaking a friendship or family relationship and speaking the truth about our limitations. I'm finding that many of our friendships actually grow when we're more honest about what we can and can't do.

People who don't care much about what other people think of them don't generally struggle with disappointing people. Frankly, I'm not there yet. I think this is harder for women than for men, and harder for moms than for other women, possibly because we're in that mode—that nose-wiping, cereal-pouring, need-meeting season of life.

I remind myself: This will not make me feel loved, so if that's why I'm saying yes, that's not a good reason. The love I want will not be found here, and what I will feel in its place is resentment and anger.

I'm committed to a particular, limited amount of things in this season, and if what's being asked of me isn't one of those, then it stands in the way. That's why knowing your purpose and priorities for a given season is so valuable—because those commitments become the litmus test for all the decisions you face.

Picture your relationships like concentric circles: the inner circle is your spouse, your children, your very best friends. Then the next circle out is your extended family and good friends. Then people you know, but not well, colleagues, and so on, to the outer edge. Aim to disappoint the people at the center as rarely as possible. And then learn to be more and more comfortable with disappointing the people who lie at the edges of the circle—people you're not as close to, people who do not and should not require your unflagging dedication.

To do this, though, you have to give even the people closest to you—maybe especially the people closest to you—realistic expectations for what you can give to them.

We disappoint people because we're limited. We have to accept the idea of our own limitations in order to accept the idea that we'll disappoint people. I have *this much* time. I have *this much* energy. I have *this much* relational capacity.

And it does get easier. The first few times I had to say *no* were excruciating. But as you regularly tell the truth about what you can and can't do, who you are and who you're not, you'll be surprised at how some people will cheer you on. And, frankly, how much less you'll care when other people don't.

When you say, *This is what I can do; this is what I can't*, you'll find so much freedom in that. You'll be free to love your work, because you're not using it as a sneaky way to be loved or approved of. You'll be free to love the things you give to people, because you're giving them freely, untangled from resentments and anger.

My knee-jerk answer is yes. My default setting is yes. But I'm learning that time and honesty and space and prayer and writing and talking with Aaron help me see more clearly what I can and can't do, with a full heart and without resentment or hustling.

A friend I don't know well asked for help with something recently. And all the old impulses kicked in. Of course! I'm your girl! Anything for you! And then I waited and breathed and prayed and waited some more, and then I lovingly, kindly disappointed her, and I'm happy to report we both survived. Baby steps.

What the Lake Teaches

This story begins and ends on the water, and our life at the lake is a theme threaded throughout. The water continues to be, for me, an enduring spiritual image.

This book, if it wasn't told in words, could be told in a map—zigzagging all over, coming home to Chicago, and then a solid blue line to the lakeshore town we love, 80 miles across Lake Michigan.

It's at the lake that I realize how far I've come, or how far I have yet to travel. Both, maybe. It's at the lake that my priorities reshuffle, aligning more closely with my true nature.

I've wondered from time to time if we should move here, permanently, to this small Michigan town. But it seems to me that we'd bring our bustling and hustling here, and pretty soon we'd need a new place to escape to in order to recalibrate. Part of the magic of the lake is that it *isn't* home—it's away, and *away* allows us to see the rhythms and dimensions of our lives more clearly.

So it doesn't necessarily work for us to live here at the lake, but I do want the way of living that I've tasted here to inform and ground how I live everywhere, all year long. The lake gives me something to aspire to—a reminder, a rhythm, a pattern. Simple, connected to God and his world and people, uncomplicated by lots of stuff.

Along this passage, my life has become decidedly less impressive. It has, though, become so much more joyful, here on the inside, here where it matters only to me and to the people closest to me. There's less to see—fewer books being published, fewer events being spoken at, fewer trips, fewer blog posts, fewer parties. And the space that remains is beautiful and peaceful and full of life and connection, what I was looking for all along with all that pushing and proving.

In my experience with this process, you have to start with the outsides—it's the only way to begin. So it starts with calendars and concentric circles, lists, saying yes, saying no. And over time you gain a little breathing room, and with those first, beautiful deep breaths, you begin to peel the next layer: why am I doing this? What is it in me that keeps things moving so breakneck fast, that believes achieving will keep me safe, that sacrifices my own health and happiness so that people who aren't me will think I'm doing a good job, in some vague, moving-target kind of way?

I tried, on and off for the first years of this journey, to inch my way toward sanity and peace. And every fall I fell apart again, having said yes to too many things. I needed more than just a vague intention to slow down a little bit. For some of us, the addiction to motion is so deep, so pervasive, that only dramatic gestures are enough to take hold.

A friend of mine told me I was pulling the ripcord on my career by being so outspoken about how badly I didn't want to travel and speak anymore. Didn't I realize the people who were asking me to speak might read my blog, and then not invite me? Exactly, I said. That's the plan, I told him. I'm a writer, not a speaker, but I'll never write another book again if I can't get out of this constant cycle of output and exhaustion.

I had the sense that my essential self, my best self, was slipping away, and the new person in her place was someone I very much didn't want to be. She was shaped out of necessity—tough and focused enough to bear the weight of my work life, when the real me, tender and whimsical, would have crumpled under the weight.

Some of being an adult, though, is about protecting and preserving what we discover to be the best parts of ourselves, and here's a hint: they're almost always the parts we've struggled against for years. They make us weird or different, unusual but not in a good way. They're our child-sides, our innate selves, not the most productive or competitive or logical, just true. Just us. Just very simply who we are, regardless of how much quantitative value they add.

It's the perfect weather for writing: gray, cool, windy. Too sunny and you feel like you're missing out. Too cold and you can't have the balcony door open, and the balcony is the very best part of my temporary little retreat home.

When I look across the street, I can see the river, the pilings, the weathered docks. The trees are old and tall, higher than the roof, almost like I'm in a treehouse, and the wind off the river is fresh and whipping. Sometimes a gust spins through the room, and a piece of paper flies off the nightstand or a door rattles on its hinges.

This last weekend was one of the sweetest yet, and part of it, certainly, owes itself to my new learning: Memorial Day Weekend in the past has been frantic shopping and cooking and menu planning, guests upon guests, plans upon plans, times and places and texts, a chaotic effort to ring in the summer season with one more drink, one more ice cream cone, one more boat ride before falling into bed.

And this year, none of that. We stayed on the beach for hours, because there's something about the beach that just brings out the best in little kids—imagination and sand and sun and yelping and tumbling around, all the good stuff. We went to bed early knowing that, with all the fun, it would take the little boys some extra time to settle down. We stayed in our pajamas till eleven on Sunday, my cousins, their kids and mine, their parents and mine, all sitting around the Blue House kitchen table, a box of donuts from Golden Brown Bakery and a pot of coffee. We made s'mores and played with sidewalk chalk. We had breakfast tacos from the farmer's market and kept the kids happy with bowls of strawberries outside on the lawn. It was slow, and it was simple, and it was sweeter than I can remember, because it felt more like a glass of water than a firehose. Pride, for years, has told me that I am strong enough to drink from a firehose, and gluttony tells me it will all be so delicious.

But those voices are liars. The glass of cool water is more lovely and sustaining than the firehose will ever be, and I'm starting to trust the voices of peace and simplicity more than pride and gluttony. They're leading me well these days.

The more I listen to myself, my body, my feelings, and the less I listen to the "should" and "must" and "to-do" voices, the more I realize my body and spirit have been whispering all along, but I couldn't hear them over the chaos and noise of the life I'd created. I was addicted to this chaos, but like any addiction, it was damaging to me.

Here's what I know: I thought the doing and the busyness would keep me safe. They keep me numb. Which is not the same as safe, which isn't even the greatest thing to aspire to.

If you're not like me—prone to frantic levels of activity, swirling chaos, fast-moving cycles of over-commitment and resentment—then you might press your face up to the glass of my life with something like wonder and a little confusion. "Why don't you," you might suggest gently, "just slow down?" I understand the question, but I find it's a little bit like asking people who are ruining their life and health with their addiction to alcohol why they think they're so thirsty.

The stillness feels sort of like walking on the ceiling—utterly foreign. What makes sense to me: pushing. Lists.

Responsibility. Action, action, action. What's changing my life: silence. Rest. Letting myself be fragile. Asking for help.

This weekend at the lake, Friday and Saturday were clear-skied and gorgeous, and we played outside absolutely all day long, morning till night. Sunday, though, and Monday were cloudy, storms moving through, showers on and off, and that cloud cover fell over us like a soft blanket, slowing us down, urging us toward naps and movies and coloring books. Lake life has those invitations to rest and slowness woven right into the fabric of our days—rain showers that send us inside, nightfall that lays us down. But so many of us, myself chief among them, have forsaken those natural rhythms and stayed at full speed, through the night, through the storms.

I think one reason I come alive so thoroughly at the lake in a way I don't at our home deep in the Midwestern suburbs is because I can feel the presence of the natural world here—in a lakeshore town, when it rains, everything changes. When you want to eat, you go to the farmer's market, not the grocery store; and when the lightning crackles across the sky, you run for cover, throwing extra lines on the boats, securing awnings and umbrellas and deck furniture. At home, deep in the suburbs, it would take something along the lines of a true natural disaster to disrupt our well-trod routines and rhythms. I like that life at the lake depends on the sky, the water, the wind.

It's raining now, and I love the sound of the drops falling on the awning outside my window, love the smell of dirt and water, love the way rain necessarily slows everything and everyone down just a little.

What kept me running? That's the question I keep returning to, the lock I keep fiddling with. I was highly invested in maintaining my reputation as a very capable person. I thought that how other people felt about me or thought about me could determine my happiness. When I see that on the page now, staring back at me in black and white, I see how deeply flawed this idea is, how silly even.

But this is what I've learned the hard way: what people think about you means nothing in comparison to what you believe about yourself. Essentially, my identity then depended on outward approval, which changes on a dime. So you dance and you please and you placate and you prove. You become a three-ring circus and in each ring you're an entirely different performing animal, anything anyone wants you to be.

The crucial journey, then, for me, has been from dependence on external expectations, down into my own self, deeper still into God's view of me, his love for me that doesn't change, that will not change, that defines and grounds everything.

I bet it all on busyness, achievement, being known as responsible, and escaping when those things didn't work. What I see now is that what I really wanted was love, grace, connection, peace.

When you decide, finally, to stop running on the fuel of anxiety, desire to prove, fear, shame, deep inadequacy—when you decide to walk away from that fuel for a while, there's nothing but confusion and silence. You're on the side of the road, empty tank, no idea what will propel you forward. It's disorienting, freeing, terrifying. For a while, you just sit, contentedly, and contentment is the most foreign concept you know. But you learn it, shocking as it is, day by day, hour by hour. You sit in your own skin, being just your own plain self. And it's okay. And it's changing everything.

After a while, though, you realize you weren't made only for contentment; that's only half the puzzle. The other part is meaning, calling, love. And this is a new conversation, almost like speaking a second language—faltering, tongue-twisting, exhilarating.

Part 2

Tunnels

We can't trade empty for empty
We must go to the waterfall
For there's a break in the cup that holds love
Inside us all

—David Wilcox

Tunnels

I've always had what I call crazy brain—a mind that runs and spins, that remembers obscure details and whirs in the middle of the night. My mind is quick and clicking, which was a gift in a classroom, and explains why Q & A is my favorite part of every event; but it also runs ahead of me quite often, catastrophizing, over-analyzing, spinning out. As my patron saint Anne Lamott says, my mind is a bad neighborhood. I'm not a potter or a dancer—my mind is my only tool, and at the same time, it's my greatest challenge, an overeager puppy, a spinning hamster wheel.

In the last few years, there has been, in some moments, a thread of inner violence inside me. In some moments, I feel such profound self-hatred, and that terrible darkness bleeds out onto everyone around me, the way darkness does.

And then at one point, the volume of that inner violence started to scare me. I could recognize it as separate from me, not built on the true materials of my life or circumstances, but more like a curtain dropping, like a virus infecting everything. It became harder and harder to walk well on those days, even while I knew they were an aberration.

I felt that in many ways I was making good progress, inching toward a life marked more by presence and connection and less by exhaustion and competition. But this vein of inner darkness remained. If anything, maybe it became more visible once I slowed down a little. Maybe it's part of the reason I'd been running.

In the springtime, we went to Hawaii—Aaron and I worked for a few days in Honolulu, while my in-laws helped with the kids, and then we spent a few days on Kauai, just the four of us. And those days on Kauai held a true magic for our family. We rented a slate-blue Jeep and drove up into canyons and along the beaches, stopping for shave ice and visiting coffee farms and watching dolphins and turtles dip and emerge again just off the rocks. It was a time of so much sweetness and silliness. We swam and went to playgrounds and farmer's markets and fell into bed at night, exhausted and happy.

We'd heard that the snorkeling at Tunnels Beach was one of the most extraordinary spots anywhere, so one day we went to Hanalei for fish tacos, watching the kayaks and paddleboards float by on the river, and then on to Tunnels Beach, right on the edge of the Napali Coast.

It's called Tunnels because from the air, the reefs look like tunnels running under the water to the shore. We parked at the base of a deeply green mountain, steep and beautiful, and then walked and walked, until finally we arrived at this breathtaking underwater lattice of coral—"tunnels" through the sand. Henry and Aaron put on their masks and snorkels and went exploring first, while Mac and I sat at the edge of the water, letting the gentle waves knock us down a thousand times in a row, screaming with glee every time.

Henry came running back. "Mom, it's amazing! You have to come with me!" And so while Aaron played with Mac, my darling eight-year-old boy took me by the hand and we swam out through the tunnels, fins propelling us silently and smoothly. It was as absolutely extraordinary as everyone had told us, deeply blue with bright coral and schools of fish darting and circling us. All the while, Henry held my hand and pointed things out to me, leading me around the shallow coral heads, making sure I saw every brightly colored fish and plant.

I knew, even while it was happening, that this was one of those moments that a mother keeps with her forever, a snapshot of impossible sweetness. I told myself to remember absolutely every single thing about it, to stay in it and soak up every second.

And at the very same time, I felt a dagger of such aggressive hatred for myself that I couldn't concentrate. I've been snorkeling since I was a child, but I kept submerging the snorkel, sucking in salty water, sputtering and gasping. I kept shaking my head, trying to snap myself back into the present, into the wonder, into the beauty, but I couldn't. The wave of deep darkness inside me was too powerful to beat back, and while I fought to be there, fully there, I was swept away by a searing-hot knife slice of self-hatred running through me.

All I could think about was how deeply I hated myself. I was holding my son's hand as he led me through the water, snorkeling at one of the most beautiful beaches in the world. And I was choking on my aggressive, almost violent self-loathing.

Something unlocked. When Henry and I got back to the shore, over the kids' heads, I said softly to Aaron, "Something needs to change. I can't live like this anymore. We can't. They can't."

He squeezed my hand. "We're on it, baby, whatever it takes."

When we got home, I went back to my counselor, talked about it with the Cooking Club and the people who know me best. I told the truth, as honestly as I could, over and over. I kept talking, kept asking for help, kept going back to the counselor, kept learning new ways to heal old wounds.

As I drove deep and deeper into my own heart, my past, my feelings and memories, a few things began to make sense. First, the ongoing chaos, the lifelong preference for busyness and ear-splitting volume: who wouldn't rather drown out that inner vein of self-hatred? Who wouldn't rather try to outrun it? Who wouldn't simply turn the knob on the stereo and let the music drown it out?

Well, maybe some people wouldn't. Maybe some people would stoop down to pet it like a stray cat, pick it up, learn about it. Those people are psychological miracles. I, however, chose to outrun and overstuff my life to avoid the darkness.

No wonder silence terrified me. No wonder I ran from activity to activity. That day at the Tunnels I was essentially unarmed: no noise, no activity, no ear-splitting volume. Just the water, the coral, my son's small sweet hand.

And so I began to peer into the darkness, that plunging sense of deep inadequacy. It's always been there. Frankly, I didn't know other people didn't have it. I thought that at the center of all of us was black liquid self-loathing, and that's why we did everything we did—that's why some people become workaholics and some people eat and some people drink and some people have sex with strangers. To avoid that dark sludge of self-loathing at the center of all of us.

As I started to talk about this, though, gingerly at first, and then with increasing vulnerability, I realized that not everyone feels this thing I feel. Some people, apparently, feel solid and loved and secure, in their most inside, secret parts. WHAT?

Well, no wonder.

I still didn't understand the solution, but more clearly than ever, I understood the problem: the hustling that had so deeply compromised my heart was an effort to outrun the emptiness and deep insecurity inside me.

This was going to have to be, as Anne Lamott says, an inside job. And so I began the daily, unglamorous work of rebuilding that strong inner core—replacing that sludgy hatred with love.

Silly as it may sound, I begin each morning by picturing a heart—like a red cartoon heart. And I train my mind on the reality of God's unconditional love for me. For all people, for everything that he's created. When my mind wanders, I gently pull it back to the heart, like a kindergartener would make for Valentine's Day—bright and simple.

Over time, the heart began to cover the darkness. My belief in my own worth, because of God's love, began to grow, like a just-lit candle—flickery and fragile at first, and then stronger, stronger. And over time, that deep pool of unworthiness receded a little.

Another way to say it: I used to believe, in the deepest way, that there was something irreparably wrong with me. And love was a lie. Now I'm beginning to see that love is the truth and the darkness is a lie.

It used to be that I was my most anxious, jittery, frantic self when I was alone and still . . . and that makes sense to me now—essentially, I had a hollow core, and that emptiness became deafening in the stillness.

So I ran and ran and talked and talked and spun circles around my life, avoiding that emptiness. What I find now, though, is that the stillness is where I feel safe and grounded, and that the frantic living spins me away from myself, from my center, from my new and very precious awareness of how deeply I'm loved. I return to the silence to return to love.

I can't hear the voice of love when I'm hustling. All I can hear are my own feet pounding the pavement, and the sound of other runners about to overtake me, beat me. But competition has no place in my life anymore. The stillness reminds me of that.

The longer I practiced this new way of praying, of listening, of dwelling deeply in God's love, the more I began to feel truly present, instead of being hijacked a thousand times a day by my wild mind. I feel all here, collected together in a wide-eyed and able way. Simple presence. Wholeheartedness. Patience. Lack of paralyzing fear.

I feel, frankly, like the kind of mom and wife and friend I've wanted to be for a long time. Most of my regrets center around getting overwhelmed or stuck in my own head, worried and catastrophizing, endless loops of proving and shame, pushing and exhaustion.

I'm thankful for that day, weaving through the tunnels with my precious boy, when the violence inside me became profound enough to shake me into new solutions. That's how we grow, it seems; that's how we submit ourselves to the miraculous, by swimming through the tunnels.

Vinegar and Oil

My friend Geri taught me something about prayer many years ago, and the image has stayed with me. She's a New Yorker—the real kind—tough and beautiful, no-nonsense and passionate. She told me that when you begin to pray—whether you write your prayers or speak them or form them silently in your mind—picture a bottle of oil-and-vinegar salad dressing, a cruet like you'd find on the table of an old-school Italian restaurant, with a plastic red and white checkered tablecloth and a shaker of hot pepper flakes.

The vinegar, probably red wine vinegar, rests on top of the olive oil, softly red, flecked with oregano. The green-yellow oil is at the bottom of the bottle, rich and flavorful. Geri said that when you begin to pray, pour out the vinegar first—the acid, whatever's troubling you, whatever hurt you, whatever is harsh and jangling your nerves or spirit. You pour that out first—*I'm worried about this child, or I'm hurt from this conversation. I'm lonely, I'm scared. I don't know how this thing will even get fixed.* Pour out all the vinegar until it's gone.

Then what you find underneath is the oil, glistening and thick: *We're going to be fine. God is real and good and present and working.* This is the oil that women made in the Old Testament, harvesting and pressing olives for this rich green liquid. This is the grounding truth of life with God, that we're connected, that we're not alone, that life is not all vinegar—puckery and acidic. It is also oil, luscious, thick, heavy with history and flavor.

But you have to start with the vinegar or you'll never experience the oil. Many of us learned along the way to ignore the vinegar—the hot tears banging on our eyelids, the hurt feelings, the fear. Ignore them. Stuff them. Make yourself numb. And then pray dutiful, happy prayers. But this is what I'm learning about prayer: you don't get the oil until you pour out the vinegar.

I have a terrible habit of not praying about things that seem too human, too trivial to me. I get annoyed, frankly, when people pray for parking spaces in a world with so much suffering, so I swing the other way . . . I'm scared and I'm tired but I don't say that; I say, "I'm sorry I'm so fearful! I'm sorry I've gotten myself into this mess!" That's the heart of it: I don't want to pray for anything that I may have caused, or that I could undo on my own. I said yes to speaking at this event, and now if I feel scared, that's my own fault. I said yes to this deadline, and now I'm tired and struggling to meet it, but that's my own fault.

I'm learning, though, that the God who loves me isn't just looking for apologies and report cards. He wants me to bring the vinegar so that I can taste the oil. He has all the time in the world to sit with me and sift through my fears and feelings and failings. That's what prayer is. That's what love is.

And so I begin, feeling a little silly, feeling like so many people I've criticized, inviting God to solve the problems I could solve in my own life with better boundaries and a little elbow grease. But I do it anyway.

Here I am, God: I feel scared and fragile, and I worry about my kids. When I'm away from them, I miss them, but when I'm with them sometimes I feel so impatient with them. I don't like who I am sometimes, and I wonder if anyone really loves me.

And as I do it, I can feel my heart release, dropping into the hands of God, who holds it tenderly. And I start to feel connected and loved, even though I'm fragile, even though I'm weak. Maybe because I am. Because I'm not frantically trying to hide the bottle of vinegar. When I admit that it exists, when I bring it to God in prayer and silence, that's when connection can begin.

He doesn't ask me to show up and catalog my strengths. He doesn't ask me to show up and abuse myself for my failings. He asks me to bring my whole-fragile-strong-weak-good-bad self, and that starts with vinegar, and it makes a way for oil.

This is one of those things I knew how to do as a child. I think we all knew how, as children, to bring our whole selves, to relationships or friendships or in prayer with God. But along the way we learn to only bring our achievements or our desperate apologies for the lack of achievement, as though God is the foreman of the factory, punching our time cards.

But he isn't. He is love itself, grace embodied, holding the fullness of who we are—strong, weak, good, bad, wild, fearful, brave, silly—in his hands. He can be trusted with every part of it, the silly and the enormous.

I've been a Christian who hasn't trusted God with her full self for a long time. I bring him my achievements. I destroy myself for my failings—I'm sorry, I'm sorry, I'm sorry. But it's only recently that I'm relearning to do what I learned as a child: to bring my whole self, without shame and hiding, without pushing and striving.

You cannot taste the oil until you pour out the vinegar. And it's okay to admit that there's vinegar—all the small hurts and enormous fears. You pour it out, letting the all-powerful God who knows you and loves you see you as you are, the scariest thing any of us can do: allow ourselves to be seen.

I've been afraid to truly be seen for so many years. And I'm relearning to let myself be seen by a holy God. Every part, every flaw, unhidden by achievement and by shame.

It's a hard enough thing for me to do with people. It's a harder thing still for me to do with God. But it changes me, changes us, as we do it. It rearranges our molecules, grounding us to the reality of love in a thoroughly new way.

I've been ungrounded for so long—attaching to whatever

I can, whenever I can, flailing around to feel connected to something bigger than myself. I attached cognitively to the idea of God. But I didn't allow myself to be seen, vinegar and all, and so I cut myself off from the healing oil, from the grounding.

You have to pour out the acid before you get to the richness, and you can't get there unless you're willing to truly be seen, vinegar and all.

A Wide and Holy Space

Try to keep your soul always in peace and quiet, always ready for whatever our Lord may wish to work in you. It is certainly a higher virtue of the soul, and a greater grace, to be able to enjoy the Lord in different times and different places than in only one.

—Ignatius of Loyola

Aaron has been a pianist and worship leader since approximately forever, since he started playing piano and singing Keith Green songs in the small church where he grew up. In recent years, though, he's spent less time writing songs, sitting at the piano, and more time reading about liturgy, church history, spiritual formation and practices.

He was bursting with energy and dreams and ideas for new ways of gathering, exploring other traditions and ancient practices. He was reading voraciously, and spent hours walking up and down the sidewalk in front of our house, on phone call after phone call with friends around the country feeling their hearts and minds ignited by similar themes.

And then two years ago, our church invited him to bring those dreams and ideas to life. He left behind almost twenty years of leading worship in huge rooms, and he drew together a small team of likeminded friends to start the Practice. I've never seen him happier, never seen him more connected to his own passion or vocation.

We began meeting on Sunday nights in our church's chapel, a beautiful, sacred space. At the center of the room is the Eucharist table—loaves of bread, slender bottles of dark juice, waiting to be poured into bowls. A grand piano, sometimes a cello.

We begin in silence, and Aaron leads us through an opening liturgy. We pray and sing; we practice confession and assurance. We learn from rabbis and Jesuits and Pentecostals and spiritual directors. We learn from men and women, old and young, from right within our community, and from San Francisco and Tulsa and New York City.

We sit in the round, and the rest of the building is dark and hushed. Sometimes we have potlucks in the basement, and on the day of the first one, I was elated—my first church-basement potluck! There must have been a full dozen crockpots, and I was in my glory.

At dinner a few nights ago, a friend I don't see often asked me about the gathering, about what Aaron's doing these days. My friend was raised Catholic but isn't religious. I told him what Aaron's created is more like the masses he grew up going to, in some ways—creeds, written prayers, hymns, practices that originated in the Catholic church, like *lectio divina* and the Ignatian prayer of imagination. I could see the wheels turning in his mind as I explained.

He said, "When I go to your church, it's like a breath of fresh air from what I grew up with."

"Exactly," I said, "and this is a breath of fresh air from what we grew up with." I told him it was like we all grow up with half a pie, and part of being an adult person of faith is finding the rest of your pie.

I absolutely love our church—it's my sister, my home. My parents started our church the year before I was born, and it's been a constant in my life, a central part of the story of my family, and of my own life. This fall, we celebrated the church's fortieth anniversary, and it was such a tender, proud moment for my parents and my brother and me. We looked at each other almost in awe that four weirdos like us got to be a part of something so beautiful. We prayed such deeply felt prayers of gratitude, and we drew close to one another, telling old stories, laughing and crying together.

And the journey of the Practice, and the voices we're learning from in that community, is helping to fill the other half of the pie, and I'm so thankful for that, too.

We attended a Shabbat service at a Reformed synagogue recently, because the Jewish tradition has so much to teach us about Sabbath. Even though most of us didn't understand a word of Hebrew in the service, we were welcomed into their community with such warmth that there was no translation necessary.

Our friend Ian, an Episcopal priest, taught us something I'd never heard, something that shaped all of us: on a rainy night, with the raindrops echoing loudly on the roof, he told us that we never *take* communion. We *receive* communion. Taking, he said, is what happened in the garden. Receiving is what will put the world back together again. Ian began his message by reading a long passage from Patti Smith's *Just Kids*, a book I adore, and it's moving to me that my lifelong love for literature and language finds a place in that dark chapel on Sunday nights.

It feels like a coming together of a thousand threads—the Episcopal church I attended in college; the longing I felt as a child to be Catholic, because being a non-Catholic in Chicago is to be an outsider, missing out on Friday fish fries and first communions; my lit major focusing on modern Jewish and Israeli writing, with a special emphasis on the Holocaust.

Poetry and music, silence and imagination, a wide and holy space for God to demonstrate his nature to us in all sorts of ways, drawing us nearer, teaching us to see with new eyes.

As a reader and a lover of history, it's so meaningful to me to balance the relative youth of my tradition with the deep rootedness of the Catholic church, or the liturgy, or the Book of Common Prayer. I like feeling connected to something durable and beautiful, something that has endured centuries. And it's been so healing for me to have a spiritual place that invites me into depth, into quiet, into silence.

The tradition I've grown up in gave me such a respect for learning, for service, for helping people and making the world better. I wouldn't trade those things, and I'm so proud to be a part of a church that's engaged in the world, that's action-oriented and smart. And it has been so valuable to add to those great things a regular practice of silence, prayer, and Sabbath. Again, filling that pie is the work of being an adult Christian—the privilege, really. Many of us rail against what we didn't get. Or we rail against what's being offered here or there, that what they're doing isn't perfect, and what they're doing over there isn't either.

But as a pastor's daughter who has spent most of her life in churches, this is what I know: no church is perfect, and the best you can hope for is that each church experience you gather up throughout your life fills that pie a little bit. And in the same way that, for example, most artists aren't super-administrative, and most driving leaders aren't profoundly tender and most engineers aren't big on drama, that's how churches are: limited, great at a couple things, not so great at the rest. That's how I am. That's how our church is. That's how the Practice is.

And the way that God has used that Sunday night gathering is one of the things I'm most grateful for in recent years. The new voices and influences that I'm learning from, the new reading and new practices are bringing me to new life spiritually in all sorts of ways—not because they're better, and not because they're new to me, but because our God is so big, bigger than one church or one way or one tradition, and he uses such a wide and holy variety of people and voices and practices, and for that I'm profoundly thankful.

Daughter

It seems to me that Christians, even more than anyone else, ought to be deeply grounded, living a courageous rhythm of rest, prayer, service, and work. That rhythm is biblical, and it's one that Jesus himself modeled. It seems to me that Christians ought to be free in meaningful and radical ways to bow out of the culture's insistence on proving and competing. Again, like Jesus. It seems to me that Christians ought to care more deeply about their souls than their bank accounts and pants sizes. But I am a Christian, and I am guilty of all these.

My faith has not failed me, but I think maybe I have failed it. Our beautiful historic faith tradition is built on feasts and holidays, Sabbath and evening prayers—a rhythmic, beautiful life with God. And many of us, myself certainly included, have stomped on the accelerator of our own lives and obliterated all evidence of that lovely path laid out for us. But the pattern remains if you squint—if you're willing to be creative, if you're fed up enough with the noise and speed of the alternative.

I believe that certain strains of our faith have led us to this spot—they shouldn't have, of course, but this is what humans do sometimes. Christians have made too much out of work in the same way that Americans have begun engaging in yoga competitions—twisted-up versions of a purer thing. Christians want to make a difference. So we do, and we do, and we do, and then we find ourselves exhausted.

In more fundamentalist strains of the faith, there's great value on happiness, constant kindness, selflessness above all else. These are wonderful things . . . that, over time, make it really hard to say things like, "I need help." Or, "I can't do this anymore." Many Christians, women especially, were raised to be obedient and easy, to swallow feelings, to choke down tears. This has not served us well. This has made it far too easy to injure our bodies and our souls in the name of good causes—there are enough good causes to go around.

Christians ought to be decidedly anti-frantic, relentlessly present to each moment, profoundly grounded and grateful. Why, then, am I so tired? So parched? So speed-addicted? Again, the fault lies not with the tradition but with the perversion of it, and with the Christian herself—in this case, of course, me.

These days, I'm not looking for more to crusade against or for, but trying to reimagine my faith as a soft place, the antidote to my addiction, not the enabler.

I'm trying to relearn a set of patterns from the inside out: centering prayer, *lectio divina*, the prayer of *examen*. I don't practice these things instead of Bible study, corporate worship, or service, but alongside them, to build an inner core of silence and substance, unshakable in the business of life. I listen more; I picture God's heart, red and beautiful; I breathe deeply and try to imagine my faith as protection from this frantic, soulless way of living, instead of one of its motivators.

Many of us who have found ourselves to be useful in Christian service have found ourselves unable, if we're honest, to connect with God any other way. We do for him, instead of being with him. We become soldiers, instead of brothers and sisters and daughters and sons. This is dangerous, damaging territory, and I've spent too much time there.

These days, I'm relearning daughter-ness, and I find it most through silence and nature. Nature, of course, connects us back to that innate sense of having been created—of order and beauty and humility. We have been made. We are fragile. We live in connection to water and air and plants and sunshine, and when we acknowledge those things, we acknowledge our Creator. Far too often, in the winter especially, the natural world is simply something that disrupts our plans—flights delayed, schools closed.

One snowy morning recently, I felt at loose ends, disconnected from myself, from God. I'd been sick, and my mind had been anxious.

I practiced *lectio divina*, selecting a passage from Psalm 8:

"*When I look at your heavens, the work of your fingers, the moon and the stars, which you have set in place, what is man that you are mindful of him, and the son of man that you care for him?*"

As those words began to take root in me, as I read and reread them, as I prayed and listened, I felt my tangled spirit begin to untangle. I felt my breath slow and deepen. I felt a part of the natural world, governed by a good God, created with care and attentiveness. I felt my daughter-ness, my place in the family of God. And I exhaled.

Yellow Sky

The sky turned yellow last night, and we watched the weather hour by hour, thunderstorms and tornados passing just south of us. We're sleeping hard these nights, feverish all four of us, tossing and turning, sweating through sheets, kids yelping and crying out from vivid dreams. The days start a little too early, all four of us stumbling toward coffee and breakfast, clean clothes and where are my shoes? And then as wild and chaotic as the morning is, just as swiftly, they are gone, and the house is silent, and I become a writer: coffee, candle, laptop.

I've always thought of myself as a city girl. I love the energy, the diversity, the noise. I love the variety of experiences, the speed and volume, the endless chatter and din of traffic, the endless options and adventures.

But as I learn to dwell in the silence of my own heart, I'm finding myself drawn to the silence of nature—of water, land, expanse. As I learn to trust the stillness I've been running from for so long, I'm finding that I crave more and more silence. I'm drawn back to the water, to the sound of the waves instead of the sounds of traffic and the blare of action and excitement.

Yesterday I sat with my spiritual director. Her name is Mary, and we meet on the second floor of a Jesuit retreat center bordered by horse farms. I slide my hand up the heavy banister, feel the creaking wood stairs beneath me. We sit in a small room with a window, a radiator, two small chairs.

On a recent visit, Mary asked me about my prayer life. She asked me specifically to whom I pray, and if, when I pray, I sense a physical, embodied presence. I'm surprised at how hard it was to put into words how exactly I pray, especially because Mary and I are from different traditions, and along the way we've sometimes found that we don't understand one another's terms.

And so I fumbled around, telling her essentially that I pray to God, some version between Father and Spirit, definitely not Jesus. More like the idea of God, philosophically—to the sovereign, divine reality. She looked confused, understandably. Could you pray to Jesus? she asked. Would that be uncomfortable for you? Could you pray to him as though he is right here in this room, a man, alive, with a body?

I could do that, I told her. I couldn't figure out exactly why I didn't pray that way, and I kept thinking about it for several days.

I talked about it with a wise friend, and as we talked, I understood a little more.

I love being a Christian, but I think sometimes I err on the side of believing in the ideals, or, on the other side, connecting with God through his creation, through the face of a child or the words of a friend or the color of the sky. The ideals and the tactile stuff of the world, yes, but the person of Christ: almost not at all. I don't think that's particularly indicative of my church or my tradition—I think that might just be me, and I wanted to figure out why.

As my friend asked me more about it, I think what might lie beneath that sort of middle missing layer of prayer is my own discomfort with need—*my* need. Jesus, when I think of him, is the face of such love, such deep connection, it makes me feel uncomfortable with my own need, with needs that I don't want to admit to having.

One confession. More often than not, I found myself praying some version of: *You got yourself into this; you get yourself out.* When I'm tired from too much traveling. When I'm about to walk out on stage to speak. When I feel scared about the enormity of a room or an opportunity. Something inside me tells me that I can't pray for things that I've selected into and now need help with. If I'm honest, my theology of prayer seems to be: *You made your bed; now lie in it.*

But in the last year, I've been tiptoeing back into need, into admitting need, admitting that I need help.

Just as I'd developed all kinds of defenses so that I didn't have to connect deeply with fear or anxiety or complicated relational dynamics, I'd done the same thing in my spiritual life: I was a good soldier, a responsible daughter, a trustworthy servant . . . but I was not a deeply loved friend or trusting and fragile daughter. In the same way that I didn't allow myself to be taken care of by people, I didn't know how to let myself be taken care of by God. Honestly, even that phrase makes me uncomfortable.

But I know that discomfort is often the way through, and so I began. Picturing the face of Jesus—a person, a friend, someone who loves me, knows me, sees me. And I began asking for help for all sorts of things that I didn't feel I "deserved" to ask for—energy when I was depleted, patience when I was spent, courage when I was afraid. And every time, I'll be honest, it was uncomfortable, like anything you're learning, awkward at first, fumbling.

I have no trouble at all praying for other people. I love to pray for other people. For big things and small things, matters of great consequence. But I'm just beginning to get comfortable once again, after many years of distance, to pray the contents of my own heart, the needs and longings of my own spirit. It feels awkward, sometimes. And it feels life-changing.

I sat with Mary again recently. We prayed together, and at the end of our time together, she leaned forward and said, "You're ready. I can sense it. You're ready to truly know Jesus in a deeper way. Start with being. Start with silence."

She lowered her voice to a whisper. "Be not afraid, my dear one. He says, 'Be still and know that I am God.' Be still and know. Be still. Be. It starts with 'be.' Just be, dear one."

On Stillness

I said to my soul, be still, and wait without hope
For hope would be hope for the wrong thing; wait without love,
For love would be love of the wrong thing; there is yet faith
But the faith and the love and the hope are all in the waiting.
Wait without thought, for you are not ready for thought:
So the darkness shall be the light, and the stillness the dancing.

—T. S. Eliot, "East Coker," *Four Quartets*

One of the reasons I believe in God is because I can see so clearly his loving and hilarious hand, guiding us to the unlikeliest of places to find the healing we've been searching for all along. Why am I a writer, of all possible things? I hate silence, stillness, introspection. When's lunch?

My lifelong love affair with stories and words has brought me to stillness, proving once again that God has both a sense of humor and a sense of outrageous grace.

The word *stillness*, of course, brings me to Eliot, with whom I fell in love as a young reader, many years ago.

The only way through the emptiness is stillness: staring at that deep wound unflinchingly. You can't outrun anything. I've tried. All you can do is show up in the stillness.

And the grounding, the healing: I'm finding that it happens in silence. I don't want this to be true. I want there to be silence people and noise people, and God mostly reveals himself to me at parties and while I'm watching TV and reading and the music's playing really loud.

I feel sometimes like the last extrovert on earth, the last girl on the dance floor, the last person to finally own up to the fact that true silence can't be avoided if you want to be a truly connected spiritual person. I've basically spent all my life avoiding true silence.

But it's in the silence that you can finally allow yourself to be seen, and it's in the being seen that healing and groundedness can begin.

When I practice silence just for a few minutes, when I practice allowing myself to be seen and loved by the God who created me from dust, I start to carry an inner stillness with me back into the noise, like a secret. There's a quiet place inside me that I bring with me, and when I start to feel the questions, the fear, the chaos, I locate that quiet, that stillness, that grounded place.

When you begin to carry God's love and true peace deep within your actual soul like a treasure chest, you realize that you don't have to fling yourself around the planet searching for those things outside yourself. You only have to go back into the stillness to locate it. That treasure you've been searching for—for so long—was there all the time.

Stars

What has led me here was not one snap-your-fingers, before-and-after change. Instead, there have been a thousand little reasons and voices, whispers and suggestions. It's like when you're walking in Times Square or Piccadilly Circus, and every few feet someone gives you a postcard or a leaflet, an invitation to something, a show or a club. Every few steps, an invitation, then another, then another, until finally there were so many invitations I could fan them out like a dealer with a deck of cards on a table in Vegas, and I realized that my answer to all these invitations was *yes*. Yes, I will lay down this frantic way of living. Yes, I will show up to the event that I've been invited to. This event, of course, is my life.

But for now, I'm learning so much through the silence, and the space created in its absence. My crazy brain has always been my gift and my challenge, and I've tried everything to lower the volume in my head, because things really do get a little loud in there.

What I'm finding, though, is that it's my job to lower the volume just enough so my ears don't bleed, and so that I can hear the music of my life.

I'm an avoider, an escaper, an anywhere-but-here with all my thoughts and feelings kind of person. While I want so deeply and desperately to live right in the actual-messy-gritty-fabulous-ridiculous present, I've got a whole arsenal of tricks to eject me out of it. My earliest escape route: stories. Then food. Drinking. Then working. Then achieving. All the things we hold out as armor, insulating us from the pain and mess and fear.

But the pain and the mess and the fear are the fabric of actual life, woven amid love and parenting and bedtime and laundry and work. When you insulate yourself from some of it, you insulate yourself from all of it. And I want to be right in it, painful or not, scary or not. As my friend Glennon says: unarmed.

I've been armed for as long as I can remember, a veritable bunker of books and meals and drinks and to-do lists—they looked like real life, but upon closer inspection they were my armor against it.

And in this season, this unabashedly midlife passage, I'm laying down my arms, opening my hands, to mix the metaphors thoroughly. I love the simplicity of this season: it's noticeably quiet, and I'm surprised to find how much I like it.

I've been terrified of silence all my life, and for the first time, I'm finding it beautiful. Aaron, of course, is a musician—a pianist, a songwriter, a singer. But his musical soul, really, is all about the groove, the rhythm. His all-time favorite bass players play relatively few notes, and the beautiful thing they make is all about the space in between the notes—that's the groove.

In this season, I'm finding so much beauty in the space between the notes. This is new for me. This is life-changing. For the first time, I'm able to stay in the space, right inside the silence, held there, mesmerized, content, empty.

If you believe people can't change, I'm here to tell you we can. If you think you could never turn down the volume or lay down your armor or climb into the silence, I'm here to tell you that if I can, you can. If I can, anyone can. I'm a hardened case, a tough nut to crack, a lifelong connoisseur of noise and motion and excessiveness of any kind. If I can climb into silence and simplicity, anyone on earth can join me there, I promise.

Sometimes I read books about the contemplative life. But it seems to me they're always written by, you know, *contemplative people*, people who love to be alone, whose lives have always been calibrated by silence and simplicity. I'm not sure that helps me.

So here I am: a girl who loves the days that scream along from start to finish, that start with loads of espresso and switch quickly to wine with lunch, and I'm telling you that the silence is becoming my new home, that the tenderness of life unarmed is welcoming me into the sweetest season of life I've yet known.

I did not see this coming, honestly.

But I suppose I should have, because God in his goodness has been doing this thing in my life for a long time—surprising me, drawing me along to places I could never have imagined.

Whatever thing you think you can't do without: alcohol, shopping, that number on a scale. That car, that secret habit, that workout. The pills, the lies, the affair. The money, the success, the cutting. Whatever it is that you clutch onto with angry fists, that you grab like a lifeline, when you release that thing, when you let it go, that's when you'll hear the notes between the music. That's when you'll feel the groove, the rhythm you were made to feel, that you've covered over a thousand times with noise and motion and fear and all the things.

When you hear it, you'll realize it sounds a lot like your own heartbeat, the rhythm of God, of life, pumping in your chest, the most beautiful song you've ever heard.

The morning I decided to dive even more deeply and honestly into the practice of silence, I bought myself a necklace with a tiny star on a fine gold chain. Something about the star felt meaningful to me—delicate, powerful, rising, constant, lighting the dark in a small but glittering way. Several times a day, my fingers find the tiny star around my neck, a symbol of doing something difficult and valuable.

I went to see my counselor, to talk to him once again about laying down all the things that keep me full and frantic and distracted and exhausted. He said he was proud of me, and at the end of our time together, he said, "What you're saying reminds me of *The Journey*—remember that poem?"

And together we rambled around an approximation of Mary Oliver's gorgeous poem—the wild night, the voices, bad advice—"*mend my life,*" they cried.

"*But then you knew what you had to do ...*"

And when he got to the part about the stars burning through, my eyes filled with tears, and I showed him my necklace. "Stars!" I said.

In the city, you can't see the stars for the city lights. But at the lake, and in the country, the stars are so bright you can practically read by them. And that's what I'm finding: when I get out of the city—the noise and chaos, the screaming intensity—then I can see the stars.

And they're beautiful.

Part 3

Legacy

You wander from room to room
Hunting for the diamond necklace
That is already around your neck.
—Rumi

Agency

Essentially, what I'm talking about, what I'm circling ever nearer and nearer to is agency. Or maybe authority: owning one's life, for better and for worse, saying out loud, "*This is who I am, this is who I'm not, this is what I want, this is what I'm leaving behind.*"

In my experience, our culture teaches men to do this quite well. Women, it seems, have a much trickier time with it. It's only quite recently that women have even been permitted to ask these questions, and we're just getting the hang of it, many of us, fumbling and awkward—really, really? Me? Are you sure?

Yes, darling, I'm sure. You get to tell the truth about what you love and who you are and what you dream about. We'll learn this new path together.

What I'm learning is that you have to stop doing a whole lot of things to learn what it is you really love, who it is you really are. Many of us go years and years without even asking these questions, because the lives we've fallen into have told us exactly who to be and what to love and what to give ourselves to.

As I look back, in many instances, I simply followed the natural course of things. And great things happened, mostly. But over time I realized they weren't necessarily great things for me. They were maybe someone else's great things, and I was both taking up the space that was meant for them and not standing in my own space, like wearing someone else's shoes, leaving them barefoot.

Along the way I've realized that most of the hard work during my last couple seasons has been claiming authority over my own life. This is not a group decision. We're not voting for "most this" or "most that" in our yearbooks. This is actually my life, and it doesn't matter a bit if it would be lovely for someone else to live. What does matter: does it feel congruent with how God made me and called me?

Some of us are made to be faster, and some slower, some of us louder, and some quieter. Some of us are made to build things and nurture things. Some of us are made to write songs and grants and novels, all different things. And I'm finding that one of the greatest delights in life is walking away from what someone told you you should be in favor of walking toward what you truly love, in your own heart, in your own secret soul.

I thought I needed to be fast and efficient, sparkly and shiny, battle-ready and inexhaustible. There was, I will be honest with you, a lot of pressure from all sorts of places. I could be those things and so I was, and then lots of people told me I had a responsibility to do more and more and more. For a long time, I listened to them.

But what I've learned the hard way is you don't answer to a wide swath of people and their opinions, even if they're good people, with good opinions. You were made by hand with great love by the God of the universe, and he planted deep inside of you a set of loves and dreams and idiosyncrasies, and you can ignore them as long as you want, but they will at some point start yelling. Worse than that, if you ignore them long enough, they will go silent, and that's the real tragedy.

What's changing everything for me is a new understanding that we get to decide how we want to live. We get to shape our days and our weeks, and if we don't, they'll get shaped by the wide catch-all of "normal" and "typical," and who wants that?

You can live on a farm or out of a backpack. You can work from your kitchen or in a high-rise. You can worship in your living room or a cathedral. Isn't that beautiful? And exciting? And so full of freedom?

You can wear slippers or heels, eat steak or kale, read poetry or spreadsheets, fall asleep to the hum of the city or out under the stars. You get to make your life. In fact, you have to. And not only can you make it, you can *remake* it.

So many of the people I admire most have lived several lives: My favorite college professor spent a couple decades in a beach town and now lives a positively city life. My friends Tsh and Kyle and their three kids just traveled around the world for a year. Blaine, an actor and a maker who's lived like a gypsy for years, just bought a house in our neighborhood with his wife Margaret and their darling girls Ruby and Eloise, and this long-time wanderer is growing herbs and lettuces, driving down roots, literally and otherwise.

We get to decide, which is both so freeing and such a beautiful responsibility. You can be a vegan. You can be a priest. You can homeschool. You can train for a triathlon. You can live in the city. You can read the classics. You can buy all your clothes from a vintage shop. You can buy a Vespa. You can learn to speak Farsi or Italian.

This life you're building is entirely your creation, fashioned out of your dreams and fears. What do you want? What do you love? What ways of living have you simply acquiesced to, because someone told you to? Because it seemed smart or practical or easy? Are those the best words to describe how you want to live?

If I'm honest, I let words like *responsible* and *capable* govern many of my years. And what good are they? Words that I'm choosing in this season: *passion*, *connection*, *meaning*, *love*, *grace*, *spirit*.

The world will tell you how to live, if you let it. Don't let it. Take up your space. Raise your voice. Sing your song. This is your chance to make or remake a life that thrills you.

This is what I see: the men I know have very few questions about who they are, what they want, what they're offering to the world, what they're not. Frankly, that certainty, I think, holds its own challenges, but for the most part, is a gift.

Most women I know, myself certainly included, have struggled to find our own footing and calling and voice. I'm so very thankful for the solid ground that seems to multiply a couple square inches under my feet with each passing year.

I'm an extrovert, through and through, and a deeply loyal person. Because of those two qualities, I've made most of my biggest decisions by committee, choosing to believe that the people I love most will advise me well, and that their wisdom will prevail. That has been immensely helpful for so many decisions. And yet.

This last round of decisions have been made in silence and solitude, and that's been necessary and healing and challenging. I've wanted the committee, and at the same time, I've sensed that there are some seasons in which the only way through is alone, a solitary path of listening and learning. This is uncomfortable for me, and I've yearned to gather around my people at every point, for familiarity and safety.

There are, though, certain passages you have to walk alone. When you arrive on the other side, the people you love most will be there to meet you, certainly, to wrap their arms around you and walk closely with you once again. But it's only when we're truly alone that we can listen to our lives and God's voice speaking out from the silence.

These last months have required more silence than any other season in my life. I've both craved it and avoided it, in equal turns, and finally realized that the craving is something to listen to, something to obey.

These days I'm pursuing regular intervals of silence and

solitude. It's almost like training wheels, or like a cast. I'm so unfamiliar with listening deeply to my own life and desires that I can only do it in the context and confines of silence—I lose track of my own voice in a crowd very easily.

In seasons of deep transformation, silence will be your greatest guide. Even if it's scary, especially if it's scary, let silence be your anchor, your sacred space, your dwelling place. It's where you will become used to your own voice, your agency, your authority. It's where you will nurture that fledgling sense of authority, like a newborn deer on spindly fragile legs. Silence will become the incubator for your newfound spirit, keeping it safe, growing it steadily.

For the first time in my life, it's when I'm alone and quiet that I feel my strength. I need more and more of it than I ever have, like a vitamin, like a safe house.

Legacy

A friend asked me to help with a project. He had written a wonderful curriculum, helping people sort through their desires and dreams for their lives, and he needed, essentially, an on-camera guinea pig. I'd come to his house, and a film crew would shoot us sitting at his kitchen table, working through the curriculum together. I asked how I could prep for it. "Nothing!" he said. "Don't read a thing, don't plan a thing. Let's make it really fresh and real and present."

And that we did. We began in the morning—goals, memories, the plot points of my childhood and adolescent years. We plugged along, sharing stories, laughing between takes. And then toward the end, the conversation turned to legacy, the end of life, regret. And with the cameras rolling and the room full of talented, kind people I'd never met, I looked up at my friend and began to cry.

"I don't want to miss the actual fabric of the interior of my life and the beautiful children growing up right this second in my own home because I'm working to please people somewhere out there. I'm afraid I'm missing it. I'm afraid I'm doing it wrong, and I want to know that I can change."

The crew held their breath. Fat, hot tears fell onto my notebook, smearing the black ink. My friend paused before he spoke, put a brotherly hand on my shoulder. When I looked back up at him, he said, "You can get this right. It's not too late. You can start again, right now."

When we got to the end of that segment, I laughed to break the tension. I apologized to the crew. "Oh my gosh, you guys. I'm so sorry. I'll pull it together."

They laughed, shook off my apology, regrouped for the next shot. As ever, the invitations to remake your life come from every corner if you're looking for them.

In someone else's city, in someone else's home, sitting at someone else's kitchen table, I knew with all certainty that what I longed for was my own table, my own home, my city, my people.

This wasn't the first invitation, certainly. I remember another, months earlier. I was at a gathering of women, mostly writers and speakers; many I knew, some I was meeting for the first time. One of the things they asked us to do: create video content for some upcoming projects. Usually, when this happens, you show up at the assigned room at the assigned time, and a nice person introduces himself. He clips on your mic, explains the goal, and then you start the interview.

This time, though, there was no one in the room, just written instructions, a chair, and a camera aimed at the chair.

The instructions explained that all you had to do was sit, start recording via remote control, and answer any of the questions printed on the cards sitting on the chair. Easy enough.

And then I picked a card that said something about my legacy—that word again. I knew what they were looking for. They wanted me to articulate my vocation, my passion, my message. I had done it a thousand times.

But something about being away again, something about the silence of that room. The tears, once again, surprised me.

"The legacy I care most about is the one I'm creating with the people who know me best—my children, my husband, my best friends. And I have to make a change."

I wish I could tell you that everything changed in an instant after that first video shoot. Or that everything really, really did change after the second. But I've always been a stubborn one, slow to change, ignoring whispers until the screaming starts.

That idea, though, of the legacy I'm leaving is rattling around in my brain and my heart. I've preferred to believe that I can be all things to all people, but when I'm honest about my life, in the past couple years I've been better from a distance than I have been in my own home—I've given more to strangers and publishers and people who stand in line after events than I have to my neighbors, my friends. I come home weary and self-protective, pulled into a shell of exhaustion and depleted emotions.

This is, to be clear, not the legacy I want to leave.

It's All Right Here

Oh, the fear I've known,
that I might reap the praise of strangers
and end up on my own.
All I've sung was a song.
Maybe I was wrong.

—Indigo Girls, "Language or the Kiss"

I had a conversation with a fascinating man on a ferry. He was a friend of a friend, and somehow the circle of conversation we'd both been a part of ended, and it left just the two of us. He told me a story that started with love and creativity and good intentions. He told me about how passionate he was about traveling and speaking, how much he loved spreading the message of his work to people all over the world, and how the heart of it is love: loving people wherever he met them, giving them the best of his energy and his attentiveness. It sounded amazing.

And then he told me the next part of the story, which is that he became so deeply skilled at making people feel loved in an instant, and along the way he lost the ability to demonstrate actual, real love to the woman and the children who were waiting at home. Making someone feel loved in an instant is so much easier than showing someone your love over and over, day in and day out. He had become a master at quick, intense, emotional connection, and with each experience of it, he found himself less able to connect in the daily, trudging, one-after-the-other kinds of ways.

He is alone now, not living with the woman who was his wife, not living with his children. That quick love cost him enduring love, and it wasn't worth it.

This is a common story, isn't it? The pastor loves to solve other people's problems, but doesn't come home with enough energy in the tank for his family's everyday problems. The writer becomes addicted to the IV drip of blog comments and likes, while her family longs for her to close the laptop and look them in the eye. It's easy to be more charming in a sales meeting than at witching hour, and it's nice to feel competent at something when family life feels difficult at best. By "nice," I mean addictive.

So many of us have taken those steps, if we're honest, because we don't know how to fix the problems we've created, because we never learned the set of skills we needed to navigate such difficult intimacy. We dive into information or work or bicycling or whatever, because it feels good to be good at something, to master something, to control something when marriage and intimacy often feel profoundly out of our control. And so, little by little, we tiptoe away. And before we know it, there's a cavern between us, easily filled by someone simpler, better suited to us, someone, honestly, who hasn't had to put up with us for quite so long, someone who still laughs at our jokes.

Part of the reason I was so interested in my conversation with that man on the ferry boat was because it sounded so familiar to me—like the story I'd heard from so many dear friends in the last couple years. I don't know if it's a mid-thirties thing, or a married-more-than-a-dozen-years thing, but it's happening all around us. And when you look at the story in reverse, you see a thousand little choices that yielded the wreckage: one or the other retreated, for whatever reason—hurt or fear or any number of things, to self-protect or to hide. And then the distance is created. The distance seems to almost always create space for another person, and then there's a whole new level of pain and violation. But when you look back at the months and years before the third person, it's first a story about distance.

And when things are hard and painful and barbed at home, what a lovely thing it is to be loved at your work, right? What a lovely and dangerous thing. What an easy escape, into people who think you're great and work that makes you feel valuable. I can master my laptop in a way that I cannot master parenting. I can control my publishing schedule and my deadlines in a way that I cannot control our marriage.

This is why the ferry boat conversation got to me, because

there was a moment several months ago when Aaron was frustrated with me about something, and the kids were wild and grumpy. And these are the words I heard coming out of my own mouth: "Everybody else likes me better than you three do."

That's what you call a wake-up call. That's a change-your-life, start-right-now moment. And so we did. Because I was on the path that man on the ferry was on. It's easy to be liked by strangers. It's very hard to be loved and connected to the people in your home when you're always bringing them your most exhausted self and resenting the fact that the scraps you're giving them aren't cutting it.

And many of us are too exhausted from the work we love to get down on the floor with our toddlers, or stay in the second hour of a difficult conversation with our spouses.

It seems to me that one of the great hazards is quick love, which is actually charm. We get used to smiling, hugging, bantering, practicing good eye contact. And it's easier than true, slow, awkward, painful connection with someone who sees all the worst parts of you. Your act is easy. Being with you, deeply with, is difficult.

It is better to be loved than admired. It is better to be truly known and seen and taken care of by a small tribe than adored by strangers who think they know you in a meaningful way. We know that's true. But many of us, functionally, have gotten that math wrong in one season or another.

And many of us were utterly unprepared for the true intimacy required for deep, vulnerable marriage. I'm fine with partnership and sharing space. I'm a cuddler and a talker. But when it comes to truly deep connection, I'm just now building a toolbox with those skills. I feel like I'm catching up to it, barely. Quick charm will always be easier for me than deep connection. People out there are easier than the ones in here.

But quick charm is like sugar—it rots us. It winds us up and leaves us jonesing, but it doesn't feed us. Only love feeds us. And love happens over years, repetitive motions, staying, staying, staying. Showing up again. Coming clean again, being seen again. That's how love is built.

And if you can wean yourself off the drug of quick charm, off the drug of being good at something, losing yourself in something, the drug of work or money or information or marathon training—whatever it is you do to avoid the scary intimacy required for a rich home life—that's when love can begin. But only then. It's all in here, not out there.

The Man in the Tuxedo

For the Guinaugh family

The phone call came on a Tuesday afternoon, bright sun slanting in the window. I was folding laundry on the bed, and the sunlight lit up the silvery blankets and the white duvet, and I smoothed the little piles of Mac's jeans and Henry's shirts.

If you'd told me five years ago—five months ago, even—that an opportunity like this would come to me, I wouldn't have believed it. I was so happy on the phone. I almost said yes, but just basically as a formality I said I needed to talk to my husband and my agent. I hung up the phone, and where I expected a clean burst of excitement and adrenaline, instead I felt worried. I felt fearful, and nervous, and like I wanted to hide. I walked around the house for a few minutes, trying to untangle my thoughts. I grabbed a pen and paper, starting scribbling.

For most of my life, I've been skating past negative

feelings, staying busy, putting a positive spin on them. I've been ignoring my body's responses—maybe I need a coffee? A breath of fresh air? Staying in it, sitting in it, noticing those subtle messages that our body speaks to us if we listen: these have not been my experience. I've been outrunning my feelings for decades, only very recently beginning to sit with, sit still, dwell.

But I did it, on a sunny Tuesday afternoon, and what I noticed as I sat in that space was fear and anxiety. What should have delighted me instead made me afraid. And I know that *should* is one of my warning signs—that frequently I pay more attention to how I *should* feel about something than how I actually *do* feel about it.

I talked to Aaron about it when he got home, and he—who cheers me on, who celebrates with me—crumpled, overwhelmed by the prospect of what this opportunity would cost our family. I thought it was going to change, he said. I thought the crazy was over.

It wasn't a good time to talk about it, but that's part of the problem—when you've created a life for yourself that doesn't leave space for talking about life-changing decisions, you're doing it wrong. And we had been doing it wrong for a long time. He'd had an overwhelming day, and we had a video shoot at our house the next day, making me jumpy and perfectionistic about keeping the house clean, making Aaron in turn cranky and short with everyone.

I asked for more time, and in the next three days, I went back and forth a dozen times. Of course I can. If I can, then

I have to. They need me. They need me to be responsible, and tough. I should. *Warning, warning, warning.* The words *tough*, *responsible*, and *should* have never led me to life and wholeness.

The video shoot came and went, then a road trip and out-of-town meeting came and went, and I arrived back in town just in time for small group. Blaine and Margaret had just moved into our neighborhood, and once our boys were settled with their favorite sitter, Aaron and I walked over, boots crunching the snow and ice, holding hands, our breath making clouds in the light of the streetlights.

Margaret made my favorite pork ragu over pappardelle, and after dinner we sat in their new living room. I wanted their advice—I knew what I wanted, and I knew what I'd always been doing, what I'd been trained to do. I knew what the right thing was ideologically, but I'm a good soldier, and I wanted this team to know that.

And then Margaret told us about a dear family friend dying of cancer. This is the very end—a month, maybe. Earlier that week, he asked Blaine to come over and record a video.

When Blaine arrived, he was shocked to see that Robert was in a tuxedo. The video he wanted Blaine to capture was his toasts for his kids' weddings. Because he won't be there for his kids' weddings. He had written his toasts word for word, and he spoke those words right into the camera, voice garbled by his sickness. He was, Margaret told us, using every remaining second, leaving nothing unsaid, giving love and words and stories and wisdom, spending the last moments he has with great intention.

They turned to me. You said you needed advice? they asked. No, I said. I did, but now I know. I don't know this man, the one who stood in his tuxedo, speaking to his children at some future wedding day. And his story is his, and it's valuable on its own terms, nothing to do with me. And yet I do believe that if you're asking for help, for guidance, you'll receive it, and it might come in a different way than you expect.

I needed to know who should get the best of my energy: my boys or a company that asked me to speak for them. I needed to know what matters. And the image of that man in his tuxedo was all I needed. You will always regret something. You will always disappoint someone. But it isn't going to be my husband and our boys. It has been, sometimes. But I'm learning. And I'm making things right.

And so this morning, I sent the email—afraid I'd be seen as weak or irresponsible, afraid that by saying no to this opportunity, I'd be pulling the ripcord on a career I'd spent a decade building, praying for opportunities like this one. At the same time, though, I knew that this was a clear shot at a new future. That saying yes to this would be continuing a way of living, a set of patterns that I've been trying to leave behind for a long time. It became enormous in my mind: can I change, or can't I? Do I mean all the things I've been saying about worth and rest and what matters most, or don't I?

I wrote the email, praying as I wrote, releasing control.

I felt more peace after I sent it than I had all week. *No* to this could very well mean *no* to another opportunity I really wanted. But I had to lay them both down, because I needed to leave this old way of living—jamming things onto the calendar last minute, clearing away space to write and connect with my family, only to fill it up at the last minute with one more event, one more trip, one more conversation where I couldn't figure out how to say no and so I said yes, crammed full of fear and building resentment.

And then a few hours later, the response came: we understand. We affirm your decision, and we still want to invite you into this other project, when it's right for you, in the way that's right for you. My no was heard, and it was valued. I was so close to doing something I didn't want to do because I was afraid. I was so close to doing the wrong thing for my husband and my boys.

But I kept thinking of the man in the tuxedo, who knows now, because the end is coming, what matters more than anything.

The no I said today is making space for yes, something I haven't had space for in a long time. In recent years, I started to sense that I was being run by something other than my own voice and calling, something other than God's vision for my life. And I talked and talked about it, but unfortunately, mostly kept doing things the same old way—out of habit and fear and that crazy sense that just one more would be okay, now just one more, now just for him or her, for an old friend, to help someone out.

But sometimes you need to say *not one more time.* I won't get this wrong again. Today was that day for me. My kids won't know the difference. Mac won't even remember. But I'll know. I'll know, when I tuck them in at night, when I make them jelly toast in the morning that I could have been somewhere else, and a man in a tuxedo, a man I've never met, showed me a better way.

The Spring of the Basketball Hoop

This spring is The Spring of the Basketball Hoop. Aaron and I had talked about it a little bit, in the loose conversation we have on a walk, or while the boys are tearing around the park. "We should get a basketball hoop" fell into the same idle well-intentioned chatter as "we should do something about the landscaping" and "we should go camping."

And then one day, when one of our boys was having a hard day—another hard day after a couple hard weeks: anxiety and fear, sleeplessness—he and I were in the house, and when we looked out the front window, we saw Aaron dragging a basketball hoop down the sidewalk. One of our neighbors had dragged it to the curb and stuck a "free" sign on it, and on his way home from work, Aaron grabbed it.

We ran outside, delighted, confused. *Did you just steal a basketball hoop?* Our son was very concerned. Aaron assured him that it was free for the taking. We cleaned it up, and put up a smaller sized one, too, for littler kids.

And we are just absolutely in love with this beat-up, hand-me-down basketball hoop and its shorter neighbor hoop. On hard mornings, it helps our son's anxious feelings if we make sure we're all ready about twenty minutes before the bus comes, and we all go outside together. I shuffle out in my slippers and bedhead, bringing out coffee for Aaron and me. The kids shoot around, and the neighbor kids wander over. By the time the bus comes, the nerves have been shaken off, and our boy runs to the corner, yelping and laughing with the rest of the kids.

We play before school and after, and it's contagious, it seems. You can't walk by without shooting, and then if you miss you can't help but try a few more times. We had friends over for dinner last night, and one friend had just finished preaching at church. He was still in his navy blazer, but he jumped right in and took a few shots nonetheless.

My brother and dad shoot around with us when they stop over on Wednesday nights and Saturday mornings. One night, our boys were shooting around, and Aaron sunk a great shot. I took a picture of him while he shot, and he posted it on Instagram, issuing a challenge to his best friend Steve, one of the best basketball players we know, and one of the most competitive people we know. We laughed about it, and then I went in to start dinner, slicing tomatoes and onions and jalapenos, scooping avocados out of their leathery shells for guacamole.

I heard cheering in the driveway—apparently Steve saw the post at his house, jumped in the car, and was running up our driveway while the kids cheered and yelled. Challenge! Challenge! It would offend Aaron terribly if I called it an upset, but that's what it was: Aaron beat Steve quite soundly, and the kids were delighted about the whole thing. We went in and had tacos and quesadillas, and the boys kept saying, "Remember when Daddy beat Uncle Steve?"

We had a party recently, lots of adults and kids, and while I'd planned for us to eat around the dining room table and at the kitchen counter, the group planted itself in the driveway, because of the boys, because of the basketball hoop. We pulled the grill around from the back patio, and the fire pit, too. We roasted marshmallows in the driveway, watched the stars come out, shot baskets till it was too dark to see a thing.

It feels right, more and more often, to let the boys' desires define our decisions—not in every way, but in some. The hours we've spent in the driveway this spring are some of the sweetest we've spent together. Aaron and I aren't homebodies at all, not routine people even a little. We love to travel, love the changes of scenery and adventure. But our boys are teaching us about home, about patterns, about the most meaningful ways to spend our time.

Our home is becoming more an anchor and less a place to land for a hot minute between work trips. Our driveway, of all places, is becoming the place where our life unfolds, and I'm loving the change.

When Brave Looks Boring

My brother, Todd, and I live on the same street. We share a lawnmower, and he stops over for a drink and to say hi to the boys a couple of times a week after work.

One night, Aaron was working and the boys were playing and Todd and I had a rare quiet moment, sitting alone together in the kitchen.

Something had gotten tangled up between Aaron and me that week. I can't even remember what it was, but I made some comment to my brother about the joys of matrimony. He's single, and profoundly independent. I know our messy, loud kid-house makes him half crazy.

But that night, he said, "I think you and Aaron are really brave. Look what you've done. Look what you've built. You've built a marriage, a home, a family. You've stayed with it, even when it was hard; you're patient with the kids even when that's hard. I think that's brave."

Todd's one of those people who's done like a million

exciting things, among them, sailing around the world. He told me that people used to always tell him, "You're so brave!"

He looked at me evenly while he spoke. "Sailing around the world isn't necessarily brave. Leaving real life for two years isn't necessarily brave. What you're doing—what you're building—I think that's brave."

His words stayed with me after he left, after I tucked the boys in, after I walked through our little house, turning off lights, picking up toys, closing drapes.

He was right, I realized. Brave doesn't always involve grand gestures.

Sometimes brave looks more like staying when you want to leave, telling the truth when all you want to do is change the subject.

Sometimes obedience means climbing a mountain. Sometimes obedience means staying home. Sometimes brave looks like building something big and shiny. Sometimes it means dismantling a machine that threatened to overshadow much more important things.

We're addicted to big and sweeping and photo-ready—crossing oceans, changing it all, starting new things, dreams and visions and challenges, marathons and flights and ascending tall peaks.

But the rush to scramble up onto platforms, to cross oceans, to be heard and seen and known sometimes comes at a cost, and sometimes the most beautiful things we do are invisible, unsexy.

We love broad strokes, cross-country moves, kickstarter

campaigns. But brave these days is a lot quieter, at least for me. Brave is staying put when I'm addicted to rushing, forgiving myself when I want that familiar frisson of shame that I've become so used to using as a motivator. Brave is listening instead of talking. Brave is articulating my feelings, especially when the feelings are sad or scared or fragile instead of confident or happy or light.

Brave is walking away from the "strike while the iron's hot" mentality that pervades our culture. Brave is being intentional about taking your marriage from "fine" to "can't live without you." Because fine is not fine at all. Fine is like a mesh sieve, enough space for all the important things to slip through, and all you're left with is to-do lists and resentments.

It's easier to be impressive to strangers than it is to be consistently kind behind the scenes. It's easier to show up and be a hit for an hour than it is to get down on the floor with your kids when you're so tired your eyes are screaming and bone-dry. It's easier to be charming on a conference call than it is to traverse the distance between you and your spouse, the distance you created.

Sometimes being brave is being quiet. Being brave is getting off the drug of performance. For me, being brave is trusting that what my God is asking of me, what my family and community is asking from me, is totally different than what our culture says I should do.

Sometimes, brave looks boring, and that's totally, absolutely, okay.

Present Over Perfect

And now that you don't have to be perfect, you can be good.

—John Steinbeck

The phrase *present over perfect* was one I first held tightly to a few Christmases ago. I remember the moment: the table was a train wreck of wrapping paper and unfolded laundry, half-eaten cookies. My mind was running with all the remaining tasks that needed to be done—gifts bought, cards addressed, bags packed, deadlines reached.

To put it plainly: my desire for beautiful, sparkly Christmas moments was edging out my ability to live well in my own actual life, and I recognized this feeling as one I'd grappled with all my life. I want things to be spectacular, epic, over the top, exciting and dramatic. But in order to force that beauty and drama into otherwise ordinary moments, you have to push and tap dance and hustle, hustle, hustle.

I was faced with a dilemma—one so many of us face quite often: I could either wrestle my life and my kids and my house and our Christmas into something fantastic, something perfect . . . or I could plunk myself down right in the middle of the mess and realize that the mess is actually my life, the only one I'll ever get, the one I'm in danger of missing completely, waiting around for fantastic.

That Christmas I chose to be *present over perfect*, and that's still what I choose today. Some days I do it better than others—it's still a tremendous temptation for me to spin out into achievement or efficiency or performance instead of dwelling deeply in life as it presents itself each moment. Indeed, sometimes I can get a little obsessive about pursuing non-perfection just perfectly. But the endeavor itself is transformative: my marriage, my parenting, my friendships, and my connection to God have all been enriched in countless ways along this journey.

This isn't about working less or more, necessarily. This isn't about homemade or takeout, or full time or part time, or the specific ways we choose to live out our days. It's about rejecting the myth that every day is a new opportunity to prove our worth, and about the truth that our worth is inherent, given by God, not earned by our hustling.

It's about learning to show up and let ourselves be seen just as we are, massively imperfect and weak and wild and flawed in a thousand ways, but still worth loving. It's about realizing that what makes our lives meaningful is not what we accomplish, but how deeply and honestly we connect with the people in our lives, how wholly we give ourselves to the making of a better world, through kindness and courage.

Let's talk for a minute about perfect: *perfect* has become as near a dirty word to me as *hustle*, *prove*, *earn*, *compete*, and *push*. Perfect is brittle and unyielding, plastic, distant, more image than flesh. Perfect calls to mind stiffness, silicone, an aggressive and unimaginative relentlessness. Perfect and the hunt for it will ruin our lives—that's for certain.

The ache for perfection keeps us isolated and exhausted—we keep people at arm's length, if that, and we keep hustling, trying trying trying to reach some sort of ideal that never comes.

I've missed so much of my actual, human, beautiful, not-beautiful life trying to force things into perfect. But these days I'm coming to see that perfect is safe, controlled, managed. I'm finding myself drawn to mess, to darkness, to things that are loved to the point of shabbiness, or just wildly imperfect in their own gorgeous way.

I'm drawn to music that's more earnest than tidy, art that's more ragged than orderly, people who are just a touch more honest than is strictly appropriate for the situation. I'm finished hustling for perfect. It didn't deliver what they told me it would.

And so, instead: present. If perfect is plastic, present is rich, loamy soil. It's fresh bread, lumpy and warm. It's real and tactile and something you can hold with both hands, something rich and warm. Present is a face bare of makeup, a sweater you've loved for a decade, a mug that reminds you of who you used to be. It's the Bible with the battered cover, the journal filled with scribbled, secret dreams. It isn't pretty, necessarily—it isn't supposed to be.

Present is living with your feet firmly grounded in reality, pale and uncertain as it may seem. Present is choosing to believe that your own life is worth investing deeply in, instead of waiting for some rare miracle or fairy tale. Present means we understand that the here and now is sacred, sacramental, threaded through with divinity even in its plainness. Especially in its plainness.

Present over perfect living is real over image, connecting over comparing, meaning over mania, depth over artifice. *Present over perfect* living is the risky and revolutionary belief that the world God has created is beautiful and valuable on its own terms, and that it doesn't need to be zhuzzed up and fancy in order to be wonderful.

Sink deeply into the world as it stands. Breathe in the smell of rain and the scuff of leaves as they scrape across driveways on windy nights. This is where life is, not in some imaginary, photo-shopped dreamland. Here. Now. You, just as you are. Me, just as I am. This world, just as it is. This is the good stuff. This is the best stuff there is. Perfect has nothing on truly, completely, wide-eyed, open-souled present.

When I was slipping out of my heels and pencil skirts—my armor for a frantic professional world—in search of a cozier, plainer, simpler way of living, I bought a pair of white

Converse All Stars. Practically speaking, I needed a pair of shoes to wear to a camp. And I needed desperately to go to a camp—to reconnect with nature and silence and water and people who knew me well.

The Chucks, then, became a symbol of the transition from one season to another. They have become the shoes I wear when I want to feel truly grounded: low-key, low-drama, my plain old self. They're like the jeans you've had forever, the college sweatshirt you can't throw away, the baseball cap that outlasted the boyfriend and has now become part of your own story, part of who you are.

When I see them in my closet, I remember that I want to live both feet firmly planted on this gorgeous green earth, that I want to be right here and right now, that I am loved and known and that I don't have to hustle or perform.

I know that's a lot to get from a pair of sneakers. But sometimes, especially when we're in seasons of great transition, we cling to a couple things very tightly—physical reminders of deep inner revolutions—and I've held tightly to these white Chucks.

They're not my first pair—didn't everyone my age have a pair or two in high school or college? I certainly did, along the way—green ones, red ones, black ones. So these feel familiar, like a return to an essential self, like I'm traveling back to reclaim something, which is exactly what I'm doing, in many ways: I'm retracing the steps I've taken across the last several years to find the woman I used to be—she's definitely nowhere near perfect, but I like her better, and I'm determined to find her again.

Part 4

Walking on Water

I have only one thing to do
and that's be the wave that I am,
and then sink back into the ocean.

—Fiona Apple

Walking on Water

Here's the thing about filters—they color everything. Nothing is neutral; nothing escapes them. The shame glasses I wear almost all the time mean that every story looks like shame to me. Every punchline, every plot twist—they're all the same: you're not good enough. What I'm discovering, though, is when I take off the glasses, the stories I've been hearing all my life are completely different than I thought—especially stories from the Bible.

At a gathering of the Practice this summer, Father Michael, a Jesuit priest and Aaron's spiritual director, led us through an Ignatian prayer of imagination. Essentially, he reads a section of Scripture aloud and invites us to imagine ourselves in the story: What did it smell like? What did it sound like? What character in the story are you?

He used the story of Peter walking on water—deeply familiar for anyone who's grown up in church. I knew this story, of course. I knew that Jesus invited Peter out onto the water. I knew that Peter began to sink, and that Jesus scolded him for his lack of faith. I knew that story backward and forward . . . meaning that I knew the actual story, and I knew in such a visceral, familiar way all the times that I'd been Peter—step out, sink, receive the scolding. Step out—longer this time! Great job! You're doing it! But then inevitably sink, receive the scolding.

The scolding's the worst part, of course. I should be used to it, but it stings every time. I know, I know—I'll try harder. I'll focus more. I promise.

And then this gentle priest read the story again, and again, and again. We listened, exhaled, found ourselves in the story, practiced the prayer of imagination. Again and again.

And there in my chair on a summer Sunday evening, I realized that all my life I'd had the story wrong. I had twisted it for my own purposes, a practice as old as the hills. We twist the sacred words to tell our own stories. We do it with Scripture; we do it in conversation. Whatever you're looking for, you'll find. If you're looking for stories to affirm your deep belief in the goodness of humanity, you'll find them. If you're only seeking stories that say the world is nothing but evil, you'll find them. And if every story you hear, every song you sing, every tale you tell is really a story about shame and about not being good enough, you'll find it.

I know this because I've been doing it for years. For me, when someone says, "I can't come to your house," I hear, "You're not good enough." When someone says, "That woman over there is so pretty," I hear, "You're not good enough." When someone opens his or her mouth to say almost anything at all, what I hear is "you're not good enough."

So, of course, that's the story I see in this one. But on that Sunday night, something clicked and released.

Before Jesus scolds Peter, first he *rescues* him. I've had that wrong all my life. I always picture the falter, the failure, the scolding, then finally the begrudging hand of help: I knew you couldn't do it yourself. Do I have to do everything?

But now I was seeing something entirely new: the rescue came first. When Peter faltered, Jesus reached out a hand before saying a word. What an extraordinary thing! For a girl who's been failing and faltering all her life, bracing myself for the scolding, enduring the disappointment and gritting my teeth till the hand is finally extended and I am safe, the rescue coming first changes everything.

And this is what really undid me: it's not a scolding at all. It's a loving post-game analysis—hey, pal, what happened out there? How can we, together, help you stand? It's so loving, so parental, so protective . . . why haven't I ever seen it this way?

Because I'm trained for shame, and I see it everywhere, even when there's not a shred to be found. But here's the thing: what if it's not there? And what if shame actually isn't in many of the places I think it is? What if all my life I've been trying to walk with a Jesus who reprimands me while I'm drowning and grabs me at the last second, rolling his eyes? No wonder I don't tell him when I'm scared or fragile. Why would I? No wonder most of my prayers sound like minutes at a board meeting, an underling giving the quarterly report:

I'm working on this, also this. Will do better next time on this. So sorry about this, again. I'm on it. I'm on it.

Since that Sunday, sometimes when I pray, I think about the rescue. And then I think about the tenderness of that conversation after the rescue. I remind myself that I'm building a new set of stories—the ones that were true all along, instead of my old set, whispering shame at every plot point.

I think of swimming with our boys, and how when one of them struggles, I don't lecture. I don't let them flounder a few extra seconds while I correct them sternly. I scoop them up, a hundred times an hour if necessary. I watch them, grab them, keep them close. When we're safe again, when we're close to shore, then we talk about deep water or clearing our ears when we dive down deep.

But before all that, rescue. Rescue. Rescue. Even the word moves me. And then the question: why did you doubt? Not: what's wrong with you? Not the frustrated and rhetorical, "Why on earth did you do that?" that a parent asks a child after he knocks something off a counter. But a question, an invitation into conversation, a way of saying, "I'm here and I care, and let's solve this together."

I haven't often prayed to a God who says, "We've got this; we'll do it together. Your failure doesn't rattle me. Your limitations don't bother me." But I do now, little by little. Because now when I step out of that boat, I'm starting to see a man with love in his eyes, a man who will rescue and rescue and rescue, and then bring me to safety, despite my faithlessness, despite my failure.

This makes me wonder, of course, about all of Scripture... how many other stories have I twisted to tell my own story? How many images of God have I constructed out of my own wounds? And what would happen if I stepped inside of them like I did this one and found the narrative fundamentally altered?

Thank God for that gentle priest, for a tribe that gathers on Sunday nights, for the ancient tradition of the prayer of imagination. Sometimes we read the same passages all our lives without realizing we've rewritten them in our own images. How much more beautiful is our God when we free him from our own wounds and tired narratives.

Tonight, as I fall asleep, I'll picture myself walking on water. And then I'll picture myself being rescued.

Baptism

There's a new trend in books, what they're calling "burn it down" stories—stories about women who hike a thousand miles or move to the other side of the world or start something crazy or risky or bold.

This is my "burn it down" story, essentially. What I'm burning down are the expectations I've long held for who I had to be, what people needed me to be, and the distance those expectations created between God and me, and between the people I love and me, and between the beauty of the world and me.

A million years ago—or twenty, really—I bought a card at the little hippie gift shop in my college town. I glued it to the front of a notebook, and scribbled in every direction, every inch of those pages. And this is what that black-and-white card said, from the Japanese mystic Masahide, "Barn's burned down. Now I can see the moon."

When I was eighteen, nineteen, twenty, I was a mystic, a

little bit of a hippie, a voracious reader, a lover of the water and the sky.

And now I am inches from forty, a mother and writer, and the more I peel the onion, the layers of selves and identities, the more surprised I am to find that the self I want to take into my future is more like the nineteen-year-old than the person I've slipped into, the identities I tried on in more recent years.

I feel a longing to be outside, one I haven't felt for years, but one that feels familiar. For many years, there were so many structures that mattered so much to me—churches and colleges, publishing houses and gyms and malls. But now I find my heart is drawn so entirely to only two places: the table and the water. Our home and the edge of the big water, the two most sacred places I've ever known.

One way to look at it: communion and baptism. I'm a table person, a bread and wine person. And I'm a water person, profoundly. All my life, I've felt most deeply myself around the table and on the shore, the bread and the wine and the water.

We went to a friend's church yesterday, and they were baptizing a baby girl named Anna and a little boy named Knowles. In the children's gathering concurrent with the service, the teacher, Debby, taught the children about baptism, showing them the water, the shell the priest uses to scoop it, the way the water falls gently onto a doll's head. She explained each part of it, and then she invited each child to practice on the doll, with the shell, bowl, water, towel. It was sweet and beautiful, and now as I sit watching this water, so deeply connected to my own past, I can't stop thinking how the water washes us, makes us clean, brings new life, quenches our thirst.

When I think about my life now, I think about Pigpen from *Peanuts*, and how as Charles Schultz drew him, he was always surrounded by a cloud of dirt and swirling dust. I think that's how I've lived for a long time without knowing it. I thought that the noise and the chaos and the busyness were always somehow finding me, but I couldn't figure out how. What are the chances, I thought? Isn't this funny?

But over time I started to realize that I'm like one of those girls who can't figure out why drama always finds her. She swears up and down she has nothing to do with it. But then you watch her trash-talk one girl and flirt with another girl's boyfriend, and you realize that even if she doesn't see it, the drama is all her.

The chaos is all me, as much as I don't want to admit it. I create it, am drawn to it, kick it up when things get too quiet, because when I'm quiet I have to own up to the fact that quiet terrifies me, that all my life I've been wrapping myself in noise and chaos the way Pigpen is all wrapped up in dust and dirt. And that noise protects me from feeling all the things I don't want to feel.

Here I am, though—the only sound, the waves breaking on the shore and the intermittent rolls of thunder, nearer and nearer. Here I am, though—all alone, just words and a dark sky, hours set aside, blank pages.

And here's what's crazy: I was so afraid that if I faced the silence I would find that inside myself, there's simply nothing, that I'm hollow like a set of Russian dolls missing the center doll, all shells and no core. Or I thought that what I would find in the silence is weak, crumbling, unable to face life without the swirling blanket of chaos. Instead, around every corner I'm finding that willingness to be fragile actually makes me strong.

In the silence, I have found love. I have found love, and peace, and stillness, and gratitude. I used to overwork in order to feel important. What I'm learning now is that feeling important to someone else isn't valuable to me the way I thought it was. Feeling connected is very valuable. But feeling helpful to strangers doesn't do it for me anymore.

The rain is falling steadily now, the horizon obscured by fog. The sound of the rain is musical, sweet, and the birds are singing. The temperature has dropped quickly, and a cool breeze is coming off the water, infused with misty rain. I love that particular chill that you get when you're on the water, and I love the smell of the earth right as the rain begins to fall—rich, like minerals and soil and growth itself. If green had a smell, it would smell just exactly like that, like the smell in the Midwestern spring and summer just as it begins to rain. And there's no blue anymore—only green and gray as far as I can see. A few hours ago, blue surrounded me on this beautiful peninsula, sky and sea in almost every direction, but now the gray and the green are complete and deep. The wind is strong and getting stronger.

It's been a rainy summer, profoundly so, with many storms right at bedtime, the boys standing on the porch with us in their pajamas, watching the dark rolling clouds, smelling the rain.

As I've stripped things out of my life—constant traveling, overworking, compulsive activity—I'm finding that my senses are attuned so much more deeply than they've been in years. Music is reaching me with a depth I can't remember since my adolescence, and poetry and nature, too.

I thought that my midlife season would be about pushing into a new future ... and it is. I thought it would be about leaving behind the expectations and encumbrances of the past. It is. What I didn't know is that it would feel so much like recovering an essential self, not like discovering a new one.

Hold close to your essential self. Get to know it, the way you get to know everything in the world about someone you're in love with, the way you know your child, their every freckle and preference and which cry means what.

This self—this fragile and strong, creative, flip-flop and ponytail self—she's been here all along, but I left her behind, almost lost her when I started to believe that constant motion would save me, that outrunning everything would keep me safe.

You cannot be a mystic when you're hustling all the time. You can't be a poet when you start to speak in certainties. You can't stay tender and connected when you hurl yourself through life like being shot out of a cannon, your very speed a weapon you wield to keep yourself safe.

The natural world is so breathtakingly beautiful. People

are so weird and awesome and loving and life-giving. Why, then, did I try so hard for so long to get away without feeling or living deeply?

A friend was visiting with his spiritual director, listing all the ways that life had disappointed him—his marriage wasn't what he wanted; his childhood left him aching for love; his career wasn't soaring the way he'd imagined it could. On and on he went, listing all the disappointments that were his life. And all at once the usually reserved priest broke in and yelled his name. "These are the terms! Now what's the invitation?"

What an extraordinary idea: there are terms. And there are invitations. Most of us don't live this way—or at least control freaks like me don't live this way very often. We like to think *we* set the terms, and *we* issue the invitations. But maturity, perhaps, is the realization that we are not handing out terms or invitations.

To be very honest, my first several brushes with the terms of my own limitations didn't bring me to maturity. They brought me to blame, to anger, fist-shaking, sputtering with fear and outrage. But after enough limitations and failures and small deaths, even I began to come around to the invitations, to the idea that our lives are not blank slates, but they're beautiful nonetheless. No. They're beautiful *because of that*, because they've been created over time, in love and sickness and moments of courage and moments of terror.

Getting older means we start to look at our own lives and our own selves the same way we love our partners, our children. When I see Aaron, I see the same eyes I've been looking into for more than fifteen years, the same mouth that kissed me first in my parents' garage and a million times since then, each one a brick in the foundation of our life together.

What do you need to burn down in your life, to make space for a new way of living? What commitments, expectations, roles, structures seem immovable until you start to move them, and find that when you do, everything changes?

In my case, to a certain extent, I followed the path that made sense, that unfolded naturally. I held everyone together, because I always had; only now I had a husband and two kids to hold together, too. I worked and worked and pushed and pushed, because that's what I knew how to do.

And now, instead of hiding in busyness and codependence and pretending that everything's okay, when I live in the silence, it makes me brave. I feel uninsulated, unarmed, and it makes me bold. Because for the first time in a long time, I'm listening to my own voice and desires; I'm articulating my own vision for my life.

Addiction to motion—or faking or busyness or obsessive eating or obsessive dieting or whatever it is for you—builds just a tiny, luscious buffer between you and . . . everything. So words that would hurt you when you're stone-sober just don't bother you after a glass or two of wine, or after you've lost three more pounds, or as long as chocolate or pizza can keep you company, keeping you safe and distant. But you take away those things and all of a sudden, you find many of your relationships very different than you originally believed. You feel everything. Everything.

It's like wearing glasses for the first time—I was six when I got my first tiny pair, and I remember all of a sudden seeing individual blades of grass where previously there was only a bland, cohesive expanse of green.

That's how it is when you leave these things behind—busyness, exhaustion, codependence, compulsive anything—you can see the cracks and brokennesses in your relationships for what they really are, and you realize that you can't move forward the way you have been, that you have to either fix the cracks or let the connection break—those are the only two honest ways.

And so I've been busy doing both—repairing cracks in some, and letting others shatter, which they should have done a long time ago, had I not been holding the scraps together.

I'm facing myself for the first time in a long time, and I'm beginning to see myself for what I am: right and wrong, strong and fragile. All the things, all in one.

Must Be Nice

Several years ago, I recognized within myself deep jealousy toward a friend. I picked up on it when I realized my constant refrain about her life was, "Must be nice." When she told me about her schedule, or her family, or her day, I felt a snarky, itchy feeling bubble up inside of me. *Must be nice.*

This is the thing: her life seemed lighter than mine, easier. More free, more crafted to reflect her own preferences and passions. Mine had gotten away from me. In my blind need to be seen as hyper-capable, ultra-dependable, that girl who can handle anything, I'd built a life I could no longer handle. My to-do list drove me like an unkind taskmaster.

And in my most ground-down moments, I looked over at my friend's life and I saw that she was . . . playing. *Sheesh.* Connecting. *Please.* Resting. *Come on.* Asking for help. *What a baby.*

That's how it starts, at least for me. With disdain. A lot of "sheesh"-ing. Because if I can discount her, then I don't have to grapple with my own feelings about her life compared to mine. But I've been down this road enough to know how well it can instruct me if I let it. And so I cracked down through the disdain to see what was underneath, and I wasn't surprised, at this point, to find pure envy.

I wanted to rest and play. I wanted to connect and ask for help, and sometimes be fragile and sometimes just stop entirely. I wanted to listen to my own body and spirit instead of feeling like I was on a speeding train that left the station a long time ago and wasn't stopping anytime soon.

It seems to me like most of us were taught that jealousy is bad, and so when we feel it, we should push it away from ourselves as quickly as possible, get rid of it fast. But I'm learning that envy can be an extremely useful tool to demonstrate our desires, especially the ones we haven't yet allowed ourselves to feel, and so I committed to learning from my jealousy toward her. I circled it, picked it up, turned it in my hand like a prism. *What are you?* I asked. *What do you have to teach me?*

When I allowed myself to tiptoe past the disdain, past the envy, what I found was longing. I was longing for a life that felt light, right-sized for my strengths and limitations. This was never about her. This was about me.

So I set to work on making my life look more like my longings, and along that path, I found my jealousy dissipating.

And one of the ways I know that I have reached a celebration point along this journey? I'm no longer jealous of my friend, or of any friend who seems to author her life and walk it out at a pace that works for her. Because these days I author my own pace and life, and I celebrate alongside people who do the same. My disdain and jealousy brought me to change my life, because I know that sometimes the darkest parts of us can be our teachers in ways that our sweeter qualities never could.

What makes you say, "Must be nice"? What longing might your jealousy lead you to, if you're brave enough to listen to it before you push it away?

Your Mess Is Mine

I'm going to a friend's party this week—a party for her child, and that means her family will be there. She texted last night to say, "You know how my dad is sometimes, right? I feel worried about my dad at the party. I feel embarrassed."

And I texted back as quickly as I could, fingers tripping: "I get it. I get him. I love you. You don't have to worry about this with me, okay?"

We texted back and forth a little, and then all night I was thinking about the exchange. I've known her, and therefore her family, for more than two decades. We've known each other longer than we've known our husbands. We've known each other since before we could drive.

But there's something so human about feeling embarrassed, about wanting to hide, about wanting to conceal and control the out-of-control and painful things about our lives and stories and families.

Love, though, doesn't allow hiding. Love invites whole

selves and whole stories out into the light. Friendship sees into us, into our secrets, into our elaborate games and excuses. Friendship carries all this mess together, so that you don't have to hide, so that you carry it together. What a miracle!

So that friend and I carry some things for one another. She knows some of the more painful, shameful parts of my story. I know some of hers. In our little tribe we carry depression and addiction. We carry parents who drink and kids who struggle. We carry abortions and divorces and drug-using loved ones—ones who used to use, who still do, who we've lost because of it. We carry eating disorders and suicide. One night, one friend whispers into the circle, "I don't believe in God anymore." And we carry that.

Because that's what friendship is. That's what it does.

This little tribe may look squeaky clean, maybe like the kind of people who have no problems, like the kind of people who've only ever been swimming in the shallow end. But no one only lives in the shallow end. Life upends us all, and there's no sparkly exterior that can defend against disease and loss and cheating spouses. We carry depression and wounds and broken marriages. We carry addictions and diseases and scars and loss of faith. We carry it because that's what love is. That's what friendship is.

So I'll walk into her party, and I'll hug her tightly, and as I do, I'll say a prayer for her dad. I'll hug him, too, and maybe he'll be high or maybe not this time. With him, to be honest, I can't always tell.

And if you walked by the party, you might think, *I'm not*

like them. I have secrets and problems and family members who embarrass me. I'm afraid, and our secrets are the bad kind. You'll see children running around and happy parents, and you'll think you're not like them. But that's because you're not seeing what they carry. I see it, though, because they're my people. I see each of us who are carrying those heavy weights together, for one another, on behalf of one another. And it's the most beautiful thing I can think of.

We're all so much more similar than we are different. Our secrets are largely the same. Our fears are largely the same. Marriages crack, addictions take hold, families break, decisions are made that can never be reversed. No one is exempt.

My friend isn't alone. She won't be the only one at that party hoping that someone she loves pulls it together for a couple hours. She won't be the only one wishing her story was different, neater, simpler.

At some point in the party, I'll check in with another old friend—I've been carrying his family's deception and betrayal and disease for decades. I'm honored to. And he carries the broken parts of my family's story, and my failures and regrets. Because that's what we do: we carry the mess together. Your mess is mine.

The Narrowing

Last night we took the boys to a new park, adjacent to a tee-ball game—dads yelling from the stands, kids running in circles. We wound through a new neighborhood to get there, feeling a million miles from home.

Earlier, I made curry for dinner—I wanted to try a jar of red Thai curry paste I'd just bought, so in the afternoon when I should have been working, I made a relentlessly spicy shrimp and lentil curry, and then a much sweeter one with chicken and broccoli and carrots, heavier on the coconut milk, lighter on the curry paste. We ate curry over brown rice and big bowls of watermelon, and then we ran around the park, discovering the trails and swings and slides. And then the boys played with Legos while I put away dinner and got the house ready for bed—one of my favorite routines—drapes pulled closed, water glasses on nightstands, required stuffed animals in each bed.

I had just washed the sheets, so I went from room to

room, putting pillows into fresh cases, smoothing sheets onto beds, pulling blankets over them, listening to the boys giggle and build.

Just before bedtime, Henry and Aaron went for a walk around the neighborhood—big-kid privilege—and I read a novel set in Italy, listening to Mac talk himself to sleep, watching the sun slide and fade.

This morning, I drank coffee and chatted with Aaron as he washed Mac's hair in the tub—there is nothing in all the world more attractive than a man who is tender with his small son, who washes his hair and gently wipes the water out of his blue eyes.

Once the kids were dressed and breakfasts were eaten, we settled on the patio, as is our new custom, and the neighbor kids came over to shoot baskets and ride bikes before the bus came. They yelped and played, asked us to watch them shoot over and over.

As I watched them play, I was struck by how much has changed in the last three years. I thought that the speed—that frantic, anxious, powerful freight train—was outside of me, and that I needed to distance myself from it. That was partly true. But truer is that it's also inside me—the roar of pressure and pushing and relentless motion. I've always been outrunning something, from my earliest memories, escaping into something, a story or a city or a meal or an experience. Frantic, frenetic, a hummingbird, a bouncing ball.

The journey of these years has been toward quiet—toward creating quiet around me, but more than that, toward creating quiet within me, which is much more difficult, and much more profound.

I'm amazed at how many things are ultimately connected: I like living in our home more when it's less full of stuff. I find it easier to get dressed in the morning when I have fewer choices.

I've begun wandering through our house, gathering things up—less, less, less. And in my closet—less, less, less. I'm creating quiet in our home, on our walls, in my own closet, and that quiet gave me energy. The simplicity feels spacious, and inspiring, like I can draw a clean breath.

I'm beginning to learn a new, slower speed, and I can feel my heartbeat elevate in a stressful way when I feel that old speed kicking up. I can do it. I'll always be able to do it, I suppose. But I don't *want* to anymore. The part of me that craved that breakneck way of living is also the part of me that was scared, that wanted to hide, that was always outrunning.

I'm learning to silence the noise, around me and within me, and let myself be seen and loved, not for what I produce, but for the fact that I have been created by the hands of a holy God, like every other thing on this earth, equally loved, equally seen.

It seems to me that some people got the hang of this early in life, that they're just deeply fine and don't have to push or prove or earn or outrun. These people, I'm finding, are unicorns—rare and lucky. Most of us are trying to fill a wound, trying to outrun something, turning up the volume to drown out a song that's been haunting us all our lives.

Good Fruit

You don't have to sacrifice your spirit, your joy, your soul, your family, your marriage on the altar of ministry.

Just because you have the capacity to do something doesn't mean you have to do it. Management, organization, speaking and traveling: you must ask not only what fruit they bring to the world, but what fruit they yield on the inside of your life and your heart.

I didn't want to admit it, but I was surprised to find a holdout of that old, terrible doctrine: if it hurts just awful, it must be God's will for you. And the other side of the same coin: if it produces fruit, it must be God's will for you.

As I laid out those ideas, peered at them and through them, held them up to the light of God's Word, I saw that they were half true at best, possibly less.

First, we focus so often on the fruit for other people—it worked, people liked it, people gave me great feedback, and on and on.

I've spent all my life surrounded by pastors and their families, and I have seen a thousand examples of fruit in their churches and starvation in their marriages and families. I would not call that blessed, or whole, or healthy, or God's intent.

Our family is not perfect, but I grew up with a dad who communicated to me in no uncertain terms that our family life mattered immensely, that I mattered to him, that the time we spent together was sacred time. I can't thank him enough for that.

In recent years, one reason I chose to write instead of working at our church is because I knew my own capacity to throw myself headlong into the immense and ongoing needs of the church, at the expense of my family. I saw too many of my peers doing it, and I knew I'd be just as vulnerable as they are—maybe more so—to the seduction of public fruit and private wreckage.

But one year I took forty work trips. Who's to say that my family wouldn't have preferred me to be at the church, home in the evenings at least, as opposed to all those nights in hotels and airports? When we speak of regrets, this is my greatest one: that I allowed other people's visions for my career and calling take me away from what I know in my heart was the best, most whole way to live. It's an honor to be invited into those churches and conferences and colleges and bookstores, and I said yes and yes and yes, because I wanted to help, because I was honored to be asked, because of that warped idea that if there's fruit, it must be God's will.

That faux theology very quickly degenerates into basic supply and demand. Your calling is not defined only by the fruit it provides to the kingdom. Another way to say it: your family and your very self are included in the kingdom you wish to serve, and if they are not thriving, the whole of your ministry is not thriving.

Our family fared reasonably well during this season. Our boys were small, and my husband is an extraordinary parent, and we are so very thankful for four loving, present, connected grandparents, and aunts and uncles who care so well for our boys.

I, however, did not fare so well. I was wound up like a bottle rocket, sleeping poorly, eating terribly, prone to weird sicknesses and pains. Vertigo, for one. I threw up whenever I was stressed out, frequently in airports and parking lots. And yet I kept going, because I had learned long ago that one's body is a perfectly acceptable offering on the altar of ministry. It did not occur to me that "stress barfs" are a warning sign.

I knew better than to let our family suffer. My regret, though, and it is sizable and tender, is that I let myself suffer and deteriorate, body and soul, and it's naïve to think that didn't have profoundly negative effects on my children and my husband. I know it did. I cared for all three of them the best I could, but the person I was dragging back to our home, week after week, was a poor substitute for the wife and mother I wanted to be.

I was not well, but I was very, very productive. And it didn't occur to me to stop.

In a thousand ways, you live by the sword and you die by the sword. When you allow other people to determine your best choices; when you allow yourself to be carried along by what other people think your life should be, could be, must be; when you hand them the pen and tell them to write your story, you don't get the pen back. Not easily anyway.

I was an author who didn't know how to author her own life. I thought that outside forces would guide me benevolently, rightly. They did not. And it was not their job. It was mine. I abdicated authority for my own choices. And what it led to was a broken body and depleted soul.

And now some years later, I know that I am responsible for stewarding my own life, my desires and limitations, my capacities and longings. I can do far less than I originally believed.

And I'm reveling in the smallness of my capacity. This is it. This is who I am. This is all I have to give you. It's not a fire hose, unending gallons of water, knocking you over with force. It's a stream: tiny, clear, cool. That's what I have to give, and that small stream is mine to nurture, to tend, to offer first to the people I love most, my first honor and responsibility.

The twin undercurrents of being a woman and being a Christian is sort of a set-up for getting off track with this stuff—women are raised to give and give and give, to pour themselves out indiscriminately and tirelessly. And Christians, or some anyway, are raised to ignore their own bodies, their own pain, their own screaming souls, on behalf of the other, the kingdom, the church.

It has been tremendously helpful to think of myself as a

part of the kingdom, a part of the church. I am not building the kingdom if that work is destroying this member of that kingdom. If you burned down your garden in order to make more room to host and feed your friends, you would find yourself shortsighted the next time you wanted to feed the people you loved, right?

I set myself aflame as often as necessary, whatever it took to keep going, to build, to help; but I'm learning slowly that wholeness prevails.

As I sit now, the sound of the waves and the boat engines in the distance, the fishermen drifting by the peninsula, the flaking paint on the Adirondack chair on which I sit, I hardly recognize the woman I was for those years, and I breathe a prayer of gratitude for this new way of living. I have been saved, and I feel all the vigor of a zealot, a recent convert.

This is what I'm finding, every day, every hour: there is a way of living that is so sweet, so full, so whole and beautiful you'll never want to go back once you've tasted it.

Do you know what it's like to be rested? Truly rested? I didn't, for about two decades.

Do you know what it's like to feel connected, in deep and lovely ways, to the people you love most?

Do you know the sweetness of working hard and then stopping the working hard, realizing that your body and your spirit have carried you far enough and now they need to be tended to? I feel like a newborn in all this, blissful and delighted each time I take care of myself, like a new skill or a present.

What I am leaving behind doesn't leave me empty: it leaves me full, and powerful, purposed and stronger than I've ever been.

I'm not building a castle or a monument; I'm building a soul and a family. I'll tell stories all my life, writing on napkins and on the backs of receipts, or in books if they let me, but this is the promise I make to my God: I will never again be so careless, so cavalier with the body and soul you've given me.

They are the only things in all the world that have been entrusted entirely to me, and I stewarded them poorly, worshiping for a time at the altars of productivity, capability, busyness, distraction. This body and soul will become again what God intended them to be: living sacrifices, offered only to him. I will spend my life on meaning, on connection, on love, on freedom. I will not waste one more day trapped in comparison, competition, proving, and earning. That's the currency of a culture that has nothing to offer me.

It is not too strong to say that on this summer morning, sitting at a fire pit on a peninsula on Lake Geneva, I'm offering myself and the whole of my life, once again, to Jesus, and in that, I'm leaving behind both my tangle with achievement and workaholism and my neglect of my body and my spirit. I'm offering to Jesus a body, a mind, a spirit, a life, a voice, a table.

Here's the distinction: *it is for him*. It is not for all Christian events and publishers and causes. It is not for the building of my brand (a term I abhor) or the wider Christian brand (another term I abhor). It is for Jesus. More important, it is *with* Jesus.

I gave myself away indiscriminately. Be careful how much of yourself you give away, even with the best of intentions. There are things you cannot get back, things that God has not asked you to sacrifice.

And at the end of your life, I believe you will account for what you gave yourself to. Be very careful that you are not giving yourself to a pale imitation of life with Christ—life about Christ, or life generally near to Christ.

I live in the very belly of the beast: the breakneck competitive suburbs of Chicago where everyone's building something, part of a church that I adore but definitely errs on the fast-paced side of things, part of a family that regularly runs itself ragged and then runs itself ragged on vacation, the quintessential work-hard/play-hard family.

But I'm out of that game, because I came too close to losing the only thing I really have: myself. I believed I was invincible, that my body would listen to my mind if I was forceful enough with it, believed that I wasn't one of those delicate flower ladies who had to drench herself in silence and green juice in order to function.

Black coffee, red eyes, old school, old guard. With enough coffee and eyeliner I could stand on any stage. But I did throw up more than is probably normal. I cried hot tears in the car or in the shower. I administrated my children more than I did snuggle and listen to them, because snuggling and listening required emotional resources I'd long since depleted.

Part of the crazy of it is that we don't allow people to fall apart unless they're massively successful. You can't be just a normal lady with a normal job and burn yourself out—that's only for bigshot people. And so the normal, exhausted, soul-starved people keep going, because we're not special enough to burn out.

Burnout is not reserved for the rich or the famous or the profoundly successful. It's happening to so many of us, people across all kinds of careers and lifestyles.

If you're tired, you're tired, no matter what. If the life you've crafted for yourself is too heavy, it's too heavy, no matter if the people on either side of you are carrying more or less. You don't have to have a public life or a particularly busy life in order to be terribly, dangerously depleted.

You just have to buy into the idea that your feelings and body and spirit aren't worth listening to, and believe the myth that busyness or achievement or both will take away the pain.

And you can buy into those things as a stay-at-home parent or a brain surgeon, in Manhattan or on a farm, whether you're fifteen or eighty-five.

And if you, like me, have also internalized some twisted-up theology that this healing and restoration that Jesus offers are not for you, that you're a server in this great restaurant, a crew member aboard this lovely ship, then you are destined to exhaust yourself, tugging on the bootstraps of your soul, lifting something that was never meant to be carried alone.

On Jesus

As I arrive nearer and nearer to the heart of things—at least as close as I'm able to get right now—what lies at the center are these four things: Jesus, Aaron, gratitude, and strength.

As I leave things behind—heavy things, things that have kept me trapped and exhausted for so long—the outer ring of this beautiful center is gratitude. I'm so thankful for what it is to be human, and for this world and how gorgeous and odd and heartbreakingly lovely it is. I'm so thankful for blackberries and peonies and newborns and the smell of rosemary and the sound of singing, especially the wild, raspy, throaty kind. I'm so thankful for kisses from little boys and the hush of snowfall and the scent of lavender. I'm grateful for Paris and Jerusalem and San Francisco, and for Three Lakes, Wisconsin; South Haven, Michigan; and the bonfire pit at my in-laws' house, where four generations of that special family have roasted marshmallows and, invariably, sung in perfect six-part harmony.

I'm so thankful for Aaron, for our marriage; for the gentle, daily, weaving together of stories and souls and bodies; for the life we've made together, the family. With each passing year, I'm more thankful. We're more than we were a year ago, and a year before that.

The temperature's dropping as the sun dips behind the clouds. I feel like I've sat on every bench in this entire camp, and at the same time, I feel like I never want to leave. Tomorrow I'll walk for coffee, maybe, early, in the cool of the dewy morning. And then I'll find another bench, maybe an entirely new one, and my laptop and I will settle in for as long as it takes.

I used to be afraid that I was hollow somehow, that I only existed if someone could see me and hear me, like a toddler playing peek-a-boo. My whole life was an elaborate attempt at never having to be alone with myself. But the invitations kept coming, grace upon grace, to leave things behind, shed old skins, release long-held brokennesses, and when I finally walked away from all those things, there I was, alone with myself, and what I found astounded me: I wasn't afraid at all. More than that, instead of being afraid, or hollow, or nothing at all, what I found was strength. I found an unshakable core of love and passion and desire to make the world better. I found focus and a sense of power I'd never known.

This is the great anomaly of it: we cling to these structures because we think they are what keep us safe—as if we're bugs who need exoskeletons, shells outside of ourselves to protect us. But when you start to understand how strong you are, you realize that you don't need a shell at all. The inside is strong and secure, and doesn't need to be shielded by all those other things—performance, proving, busyness. There is nothing left to be shed, and at the center is strength, gratitude, Jesus.

I'm practicing that last part, to be honest. For reasons I still don't totally understand, the idea that the person of Christ is sitting next to me, bodily, keeping me company, breathing in and out as I do—it's still tricky for me. And it's still tricky for me to hand him all my silly human concerns—little wounds and worries, dreams and discouragements. But I spend more and more time sitting with him, not with the Platonic ideal of divinity, abstracted away to a safe distance. I sit with Jesus, the human-and-divine being sent to be with us, Emmanuel. I practice being with him. It feels as awkward as I'm making it sound, I'm sure. It feels sort of like if you told me a nice bunny rabbit was sitting next to me, and it adored me, and all I had to do was tell it everything, because the bunny is all-powerful.

I don't mean that in any disrespectful way, of course. I'm learning, minute by minute that I spend sitting with him, allowing myself to be heard, my heart held, my dreams known. We're in uncharted territory now, so I don't know exactly how things shift from here, but I'm finding that my ability to sit with Jesus makes me more present and connected with Aaron, with my boys. As I create space and imagination within myself to be heard by the actual person of Christ, my capacity to hear the people I love is increasing. And my sense of strength, deep inside myself, grows and grows.

So much of life seems to be about reclaiming. Creativity, of course, is so easy and natural for children, and most adults struggle to recover that wild courage to make and imagine and play. And I'm learning that spiritual practice is a reclaiming, too. I used to know how to do this kind of prayer, when I was a child, when so many voices weren't yelling their bad advice at me while I prayed, telling me I'm doing it wrong in a thousand different directions.

Here's the thing: I might be doing it wrong, in someone else's view. But as I sit, my heart grows more compassionate. My gratitude increases. I become more humble, more thankful, less fearful. So maybe there isn't a wrong on this one, so long as it's yielding a God-ward heart. And at the end of it all, at the center of it all, that's the whole of who I am: this God-ward heart. Amen.

Part 5

Living in Time

The greatest tragedy of human existence is not to live in time, in both senses of the word.

—Christian Wiman, *My Bright Abyss*

Clearing Away

Of all the things I'm learning to leave behind, one of the heaviest is the opinion of others.

One of the peculiarities of being a writer is that your work is judged and measured publicly all the time. This many stars. This many books sold. Reviews and criticisms, detailed speaker evaluations. There is no shortage of opinions.

Writing is such good training for the rest of life, if you allow it to be, because it forces you to get comfortable with failure, with the wide range of impossible-to-meet expectations and standards. I hear all the time that I'm both too conservative and too liberal, too shallow and too deep, too casual and too formal.

When our closest friends gather around our table, we do not all agree about theology. Or politics. Or education. Or almost anything at all, and that's just as it should be. Friendship isn't forged out of sameness, and anyone who has in-laws knows that family isn't either.

If our dinner tables represent great diversity of thought and opinion, imagine how much more diverse our churches and neighborhoods are, let alone the wild west of the Internet.

Some of what I'm leaving behind in this season is the need to please everyone. I want to respect all people. I want to learn from all people, most especially people who are different from me and who disagree with me, but pleasing, for me, is over.

Pleasing is such a fraught and freighted word, it seems, saccharine and over-sweet. Let's do so much more than simply please people. Let's see them and love them and delight them, look deeply into their eyes. Pleasing is a shallow and temporary joy, not nearly as valuable or rich as seeing or connecting or listening. Pleasing feels like corn syrup, like cheap candy, while pleasure is homemade pie, rich with butter, thick with sugar and ripe fruit.

For years, I have bridged that gap between differing opinions, tempered my own, made sure that everyone in the room was happy and fed and taken care of. It began as a clean love for hospitality, but over the years, I think, it devolved into care-taking and people-pleasing at the expense of my own self, at the expense of telling the truth about what I think and what I need and what matters most to me.

These days I want to love deeply and well, and that's really different from pleasing. Love is often quieter, and it's never connected to that anxious proving and tap-dancing that so many of us have learned to keep people happy.

After a lifetime of believing that the voices that mattered

were Out There, approving or disapproving of me, I'm learning to trust the voice within, the voice of God's Spirit, the whisper of my own soul. And when you learn to listen to that voice, the screaming of the crowd matters less. In some blessed moments, it matters not at all.

People, individual people, matter more to me than ever. I'm giving more focused time to the people I love than I ever have: eye to eye, uninterrupted, deeply connected. But People—as in What People Think, that nameless, faceless swamp of opinions—has less to say to me now than it ever has. And the freedom in that is astounding.

Learning to Play

One of my new things (of which there are many these days—I feel sort of adolescent, changing and growing and trying new things faster than I can keep up with, in a good way) is playing.

Playing: spending time lavishly, staring into space, wandering around the block, sitting on the kitchen floor eating blueberries with Mac.

My goal upon returning to real life after lake life is to keep my summer heart—my flexible, silly, ready-to-play, ever-so-slightly irresponsible heart. What I've been delighted to find is that it's not that our real life is all wrong, by any means—it's not that I'm doing work I hate or that I'm ill-fit for the life we've made.

It's that for all sorts of reasons, I default to hustle mode all too often.

Hustle is the opposite of heart.

And so one of the tiny little things I'm learning to do

is to play—essentially, to purposely waste time. Strategically avoid strategy, for five minutes at a time. Intentionally not be intentional about every second. Have no purpose—on purpose.

There are lots of conversations right now about how to do everything better/faster/smarter, how to streamline, multitask, layer, balance, flow, juggle. How to monetize, strategize, and on and on. This is good stuff. Necessary stuff.

But my jam these days is wasting time, playing, becoming aware of that internal engine that always wants to go faster, faster, faster. That engine is not the best part of me. My heart is the best part of me.

And I'm finding that my heart loves to play. My heart loves to color and draw, loves to dance in the kitchen, loves to shoot baskets, loves to do cartwheels with my nieces in the front yard.

What would our lives be like if our days were studded by tiny, completely unproductive, silly, nonstrategic, wild and beautiful five-minute breaks, reminders that our days are for loving and learning and laughing, not for pushing and planning, reminders that it's all about the heart, not about the hustle?

Morning and Evening

I've always stayed up later than I should, wringing the last moments out of the day, pouring the last glass of wine from the bottle, reading one more chapter, having just one more conversation. One year in my twenties, one of my New Year's resolutions was to stop sleeping in my clothes. I had a terrible habit of just falling into bed, jeans and all, and I was determined to stop that, because it seemed highly adolescent. Several years later, in my thirties, I made another New Year's resolution: to start really taking care of my face—meaning, stop using baby wipes and start using real cleanser and moisturizer like a grown-up lady. I do it sometimes, to be honest.

And then last year, my friend Emily—and Arianna Huffington—taught me to wear proper pajamas, and I consider it a breakthrough of sorts. Emily and I went to England together—the first few nights near Windsor for a speaking event for me, and then a night in London at the Dean Street Townhouse, which we both agreed was one of the very loveliest hotels ever.

In the middle of the first day, after flying all night, going straight into meetings, then having a break to nap before speaking that night, we went back to the hotel. I put on leggings—the same ones I'd wear if we went for a walk. And a T-shirt—the same one I'd wear if we went for a walk. Emily put on crisp striped cotton pajamas, a matching top and bottom. And I coveted them.

I'd just read Arianna Huffington's fantastic book *Thrive*, and she makes a point that we should all wear pajamas, and that the epidemic of wearing workout clothes to bed (especially women) has to end. Our bodies listen to what we put on them, she says. So when it's time to rest, tell your body it's time to rest by putting on your pajamas—clothes specifically made for private spaces, for quiet, for sleep. Don't confuse your body by dressing it the same way you would to go to the gym, or to coffee.

After we returned from London, I bought my first real pair of pajamas in years: navy cotton with red piping, like an old man—an old English man, maybe. I adored them. I've got polka-dotted flannel ones now, too, for winter, and a light-blue set with my monogram on the pocket. I have absolutely, fully converted to pajamas, because after a lifetime of sleeping first in jeans and a full face of makeup, then yoga pants and a hoodie, I'm finally learning to rest my body and my mind in loving, peaceful ways. I'm learning that it matters. I used to put pajamas and night cream in the same fussy-fancy category as, you know, self-care.

But all my force and pushing brought me to the end of

myself quite dramatically; brought me to poor health, isolation, exhaustion, resentment. So here I am, self-care, pajamas, night cream, all of it.

I'm also learning to leave sort of a sacred margin at the beginning and end of the day, to go to bed earlier and wake up earlier, letting the transitions between sleeping and waking and the reverse be a little gentler. Like so many things, I'm bringing the lake way of living into the rest of the year.

At home, I never think to begin and end my days outside, but at the lake, it seems so natural to walk straight out to the porch with my coffee in hand, and also so fitting to end the day there, watching the blue sky fade to pink, watching the last beachgoers straggle back to their cars, pulling wagons and pushing strollers, wet towels around their necks, feet sandy and hair messy.

It feels fitting to spend the opening and closing margins of the day on the porch, which is essentially the perfect in-between space—not inside, not fully outside. Not privately tucked inside the home, but not on a city street, entirely public.

When I begin the day in quiet on the porch, it connects me to God through prayer, and it connects me to God through his creation. There's something wonderful and healthy and healing about being outside, something my own life is crying out for. Being outside reminds me of life and God and growth, and the energy and motion of nature, all things I forget so easily when I spend my life too much indoors, too much in a world of laptops and laundry and lists.

I don't rush outside every single morning, tearing down the driveway in our decidedly suburban neighborhood. But more often than not, in the first few moments out of bed, at the very least, I open the front door, and I breathe in the fresh air. For many months of the year, it's achingly cold, and I slam the door almost immediately, cursing and shivering. But I love the reminder that there is a whole wild world out there, animals and trees and moon. I try to breathe a few deep breaths of that bitter cold air, hopping from foot to foot, wind cutting through my flannel pajamas. I think about God and creation and all the wild and wonderful things that he's made, that he's making. I feel small, and I feel a part of it all, and I feel thankful, more than ever, for another day.

Simplicity

One thing I love about both the Catholic and Jewish traditions is how connected both are to real, touchable, material life. Evangelical/Protestant Christianity so often severs the connection between sacred and material, but I believe that's both an artificial and an unhelpful dichotomy. What we own, what we touch, what we carry: these things matter. What we surround ourselves with, how we regard our material possessions and our physical selves: these things matter.

I've always known this, but I'm learning it in all new depths this season. As I've been aching for simplicity inside myself—in my heart, in my spirit—I've been surprised to find how much simplifying my material world has created space not just around me, but inside me.

In preparation for a long international trip recently, I packed pink and red and blue shirts, jeans, leggings, boots. And even though I dragged a rainbow of clothes halfway across the world, every morning, all I wanted to wear was white, black, gray, and blue. The same is generally true at home—I always feel most comfortable in neutrals and blues, and my friends tease me about how often I wear stripes—navy and white, black and white, over and over.

I think my preference for only neutrals and blues struck me more forcefully on this trip for two reasons: first, because I kept having to pack and repack all these brightly colored things I wasn't even wearing, and second, because I was trying so hard to find simplicity in so many areas of life, and this one was sort of staring me in the face, waiting for me to catch on.

When I got home from the trip, I returned the pink and red and green shirts I'd carried thousands of miles, having never even removed the tags. I cleaned out my closet, selling and donating bags and bags of things—colors I didn't wear even though I thought I should, shapes that someone would love but I didn't. And when I was finished, I felt lighter, more like myself.

For some people, getting dressed is a delight, a way to tell the world who they are, a creative and inspiring process. Some people get a little charge of energy from the pure variety of what they buy and put together and wear. I'm finding that I get a little charge of energy from knowing exactly what I love and what I don't, and being clear about the two. I'm more inspired by a near-uniform, a narrow set of parameters that make me feel most like myself.

I love wearing black, white, gray, and blue. I love classic shapes, stripes, jeans. And I love the flash of metallics, like gold sandals and jewelry. I find such delight and energy in this newly simple way of dressing—that actually I'd been practicing for a long time, only now my closet reflected it.

I've been doing the same thing in my kitchen for several years, and the simplicity and focus brings me great joy. When we moved from Grand Rapids back to Chicago, I brought dishes upon dishes. I was never a crazy clothes shopper, or even a wild accumulator of home stuff, but dishes were my absolute downfall. I had sets upon sets, half sets, specialized sets—four bowls and a serving bowl for pasta, dozens of tiny dessert plates, a truly insane amount of champagne flutes I'd accumulated over the years, mismatched and colorful.

My dear cousin persuaded me to part with everything that wasn't white, glass, silver, or wood, with the exception of my red Le Creuset cookware—the kitchen equivalent of my love for blue clothing. We boxed up green and purple dishes, hand-painted harlequin-print serving ware, a whole set of lavender enameled-tin plates and bowls, and kept only white plates, clear juice glasses, and white serving platters.

My cousin promised that the simplicity of it would bring me joy, and it absolutely did. Our kitchen since then has been filled only with things we use and love, things that all go together, things that are easily and cheaply replaced if they break.

In the kitchen, in the closet, and throughout the rest of the house, I kept finding that the more I let go of, the happier I was. It almost seemed like the less stuff there was in our home, the more freely I could breathe, the more deeply I was able to think.

It makes sense to me, because, as in so many other areas, I've always loved the way we interact with our stuff at the lake. It's easier, of course, to live with simplicity in a house that's not yours for a couple weeks at a time, but I do find when I'm there, I don't miss all our stuff. I like having just a few dresses, flip-flops, shorts. I like a bin or two of toys, one stack of books. I like having one candle that I bring from home, two boxes of tea, Aaron's guitar and Henry's colored pencils, and little else cluttering up the house.

Of course it's easy to live simple just for a short season, in a home that's not yours, but every August when we return home, I'm amazed by all our stuff, and invariably, as we unpack, I also pack up boxes and boxes of things that lake life has taught me are inessential, and I breathe more deeply as I do.

My love for dishes is only rivaled by my love for books, and for a while, in our home, we had them in every room, including the guest bathroom, and even stacked in every inch of a nonworking fireplace. Stacks of books as end tables, on the back of the toilet, in the kids' rooms, a couple on every step leading down to the basement. But: lightness. But: simplicity. And so one sunny morning, Mac and I took more than twenty boxes to a used bookstore. I kept only books that I would reread or recommend wholeheartedly to a friend, and that still left a lot, but twenty boxes out the door did indeed make a big difference.

The other benefit I'm finding in these newer, narrower parameters about what I wear and what fills my cabinets is that I'm finding I make better decisions when I make fewer decisions. When I open my closet and see only things I love, and relatively few of them, when I open my cabinets and see nothing but white plates, those are just that many fewer decisions to make in a day that always, invariably, make that day just a couple ticks easier, and I'll take it.

I'm able to give more focused attention on the higher-stakes decisions in my life—the ones about parenting, marriage, friendship—when I don't have to think hard about what to wear or how to manage all my stuff. The ambient noise of my life gets quieter when there's less stuff in my life, and fewer decisions to make about that stuff. And in the newfound silences is space for connection, rest, listening, learning.

I find myself filling my cart and my shopping bag differently these days, too—do I want to manage this? Clean this? Find a place for this? Will this bring me ongoing joy, or will it be just another thing to store, just another thing to clutter up my mind and home? I'm bringing fewer and fewer things into our home, and I'm shopping for other people in new ways, too—what are timeless, useful gifts, instead of easy-to-pick-up knickknacks? Or even better, what experiences can we share, instead of what items can I fill their home with?

These days, Aaron and I go for walks, meals, trips. We used to buy each other jewelry or golf clubs, respectively. Now we buy games to play with the kids, tickets to shows, trips to cities we love, and our marriage is the richer for it.

It's been said a million times that the most important things aren't things. But if we're not careful, it seems, many of us find ourselves overwhelmed by all the stuff we have to manage, instead of focused on what we're most passionate about—writing or making or painting or connecting with people.

I want the stuff in my life to be light, easily managed, simple, so that the best of my energy is free for people, dreams, creativity; so that we can make memories around the table, eating meals served on those white plates; so that I can run after my kids in one of a half-dozen striped shirts; so that when you want to borrow a book, each one on my shelf tells a meaningful story.

How we live matters, and what you choose to own will shape your life, whether you choose to admit it or not. Let's live lightly, freely, courageously, surrounded only by what brings joy, simplicity, and beauty.

Happy Medium

What it seems the world wants me to be: really skinny and really tired. If I could shrink and hustle, I'd be right there, skinny and tired. Shrink and Hustle. This is what our culture wants women to be: skinny and tired, from relentlessly shrinking and hustling.

To be clear, I have nothing against people who are really skinny, whether that's just how God made their bodies or because fitness and nutrition are central parts of their lives. You do you, skinny people.

But I'm going to do me, and me is not skinny. I'm just not. And I've lived all my life, nearly forty years, believing a fantasy that I'm just about six months from finally being skinny. *Okay, six more months. Six more. Oops. I don't know what I was doing the last six months, but six months from now, for sure.*

You know what? Six months from now, I bet I'm going to look pretty much like this. How do I know? Because I've basically been this size since I was fourteen years old. I think my body is trying to tell me something, and essentially it's this: *Hey, crazy lady, this is what God gave you. And you're sort of the last to know.*

And so at long last, I'm making peace with medium. And choosing to be happy. Rested, not exhausted, not afraid, not wired and panicky all the time. This is countercultural. This is rebellious.

What I want so deeply, and what I want to offer you: grace and nourishment. And those are the exact opposites of what I've been practicing for so long: exhaustion and starvation.

This is hospitality at its core. This is the beat of my heart: to experience grace and nourishment, and to offer it, one in each hand, to every person I meet—grace and nourishment. You can rest. You don't have to starve.

The messages of the world say, in no uncertain terms: ruin yourself, and starve yourself. Wring yourself out. Ignore your hunger, your soul, your sickness, your longing.

Exhaustion and starvation are the twin virtues of that world, but I will not live there anymore.

I will practice hospitality—the offering of grace and nourishment—to myself. Instead of being starved and small, I will be medium. And I will be happy.

Or actually, maybe not. Maybe I won't be happy all of the time. Maybe when I'm sixty, instead of forty, I'll be able to be happy with my size, with my flesh. But of course *this is exactly the point*: hospitality, not perfection. I'll show hospitality even to the fact that I am sometimes unhappy with my body. Unhappiness, come right in, sit right down. We'll sit together. You'll stay until you tire of this, and go.

I will practice hospitality to my very own body—you can rest, you can be nourished, you can be loved. And I'll also practice hospitality to my complicated feelings about my body. Because they're a part of me, too.

Some of my obsession with perfection rears its head on this topic. I don't often these days expect my body to be perfect. But I do sometimes demand my outlook about it to be perfectly evolved and positive. I'm not there yet.

I'm going to both take up space and create space—for my body, and also for my sadness and my longing and my anger. There's room here for good days and bad ones, for crying in dressing rooms and dancing in the kitchen. For sizing up my jeans . . . again, and for feeling something like beautiful when my husband captures a photo of me on the beach with our boys.

I really wanted to have this part of my life nailed by the time I turned forty. I suppose I still could—we have a couple months. But I think this is one I might not ever nail. It might be one I just learn to make space for in my life and my heart.

Here's to being medium. And here's to sometimes being happy about it, and to giving myself space and grace when I'm not.

On Snow

God's voice thunders in marvelous ways; he does great things beyond our understanding. He says to the snow, "Fall on the earth," and to the rain shower, "Be a mighty downpour."

Job 37:5–6

I love the freedom and grace that flood through me when I read this passage from Job.

God says to the snow, "Fall on the earth." That's it. Just do one thing. Just fall. And then he says to the rain shower, "Be a mighty downpour." Essentially, he's saying: just do the thing I've actually created you to do. You're rain: so rain. You're snow: so snow.

I love the simplicity of that, the tremendous weight that takes off my shoulders. God's asking me to be the thing he's already created me to be. And he's asking you to be the thing he's already created for you to be.

He doesn't tell the snow to thaw and become rain, or the rain to freeze itself into snow. He says, essentially: do your thing. Do the thing that you love to do, that you've been created to do.

So many of us twist ourselves up in knots trying desperately to be something else, someone else, some endless list of qualities and capabilities that we think will make us loved or safe or happy. That's an exhausting way to live, and I know that because I've done it.

God tells the rain to just pour down. He tells the snow to simply fall. What are the things that he's asking you to do, the things he made you to do, the things you do effortlessly and easily?

What do you do with the ease and lightness of falling snow? Many of us have wandered so far from those things. We've gotten wrapped up in what someone else wanted us to be, what we thought would keep us happy and safe and gain us approval.

But there's tremendous value in traveling back to our essential selves, the loves and skills and passions that God planted inside us long ago.

When I look at my life these days, I see the threads of passion and identity that I've carried through my whole life: books and reading, people and connection, food and the table. These are the things I've always loved, and they continue to bring me great joy and fulfillment.

Think about your adolescent self, your child self, the "you" you've always been. God imprinted a sacred, beautiful collection of passions and capacities right onto your heart: what do you love? What does your passion bubble over for?

So much of adulthood is peeling off the layers of expectation and pressure, and protecting those precious things that lie beneath. We live in a culture that shouts, that prescribes rather narrowly what it means to be a woman, what it means to be a success, what it means to live a valuable life.

But those definitions require us to live on a treadmill, both literally and figuratively, always hustling to fit in, to be thin enough and young enough and sparkly enough, for our homes to be large and spotless, our children well-mannered and clean-faced, our dreams orderly and profitable. But that's not life. That's not where the fullness of joy and meaning are found.

The snow is only meant, created, commanded to fall. The rain is only meant, created, commanded to pour down. You were only meant, created, commanded to be who you are, weird and wonderful, imperfect and messy and lovely.

What do you need to leave behind in order to recover that essential self that God created? What do you need to walk away from in order to reclaim those parts of you that God designed, unique to you and for his purposes?

Part 6

Throwing Candy

When we are who we are called to be,
we will set the world ablaze.

—St. Catherine of Siena

Throwing Candy

I had an experience a couple summers ago that changed everything for me. That sounds hyperbolic, I know. But every once in a while we have these experiences that slice our lives into *before* and *after*, and this was one of those for me.

A friend of a friend invited me on a trip. To a place I'd never been, with a group of people most of whom I'd never met. I didn't know what to expect, but I did have this sense that there was something waiting for me there—something I needed to learn. A conversation, a lesson, a moment.

There was lots of space and silence. The stars were so bright, and the layers and layers of stress and regret and toughness I'd been wearing for ages slipped off one by one, until there I was, just me.

And without that shell, it's like I could feel everything and see everything with such clarity. It was like Technicolor, and I knew that there was something important there for me to see. I could sense it. For the first time in a long time, I was really paying attention.

One of the traditions of this place is that when you see kayakers in the water paddling by from the nearby camp, no matter what you're doing, you stop and throw candy to them. Because it's fun. Because it's a sweet tradition. Because it makes people happy.

If you knew me ten years ago, you'd say, that kind of thing is *so Shauna*. She's totally the candy-throwing type. But to be honest, I don't know if you'd say that about me the last couple years.

One afternoon, the kayakers crossed in front of our dock while about a million other things were happening. Two large powerboats were docking, as well as a sailboat, and a few paddle boarders were trying not to get in the way. There were swimmers in the water. All at the same time, in a relatively small space.

But the man who was in charge of it all, our host—the one who was responsible for everyone, who owned all the stuff that was about to crash in about a thousand ways—stopped what he was doing and sprinted down the dock to get the lollipops.

I had a little panic attack, because what he was doing seemed so irresponsible (warning word: *irresponsible*). He threw candy, right in the middle of it. Everything swirled around him, and he kept throwing candy, over and over, handful after handful.

And everything was fine. All the boats were docked safely, the swimmers were fine, nothing happened.

As I watched from the deck of the lodge, I put my head down on the wide railing, and I began to sob.

Because I used to throw candy, right in the middle of it all. I used to throw candy no matter what. I used to be warm and whimsical. I used to believe in the power of silliness and memory-making and laughter.

And then I became the kind of person who threw candy as long as nothing else was going on—as long as it didn't get in the way of being responsible. I threw candy at approved and sanctioned candy-throwing time, after all the work was done and things were safe and lunches were made.

And then I got so wrapped up in being responsible that it was never the right time to throw candy.

And then, the worst thing: I became the kind of person who made fun of candy-throwers . . . please—who has time? What is this, kindergarten? I've got a list, people, and a flight to catch.

What a loss—for me, for my family, for our community, for all the joy and laughter and silliness we missed out on because I was busy being busy.

These are the hardest changes I've made in a long time. And they're the most valuable. I'm never going back there. I'm done with that kind of responsible. I don't want to get to the end of my life and look back and realize that the best thing about me was I was organized. That I executed well, that I ran a tight ship, that I never missed a detail. I want to look back and remember all the times I threw candy, even when it didn't make sense. *Especially* when it didn't make sense.

I know how hard it is to juggle everything. I'm right in it, with little kids and a full-time job and dreams for the future and regrets about the past.

And that's why I'm throwing candy every chance I get.

Essential Self

You find peace not by rearranging the circumstances of your life, but by realizing who you are at the deepest level.

—Thomas Merton

I drove up to Lake Geneva for a few days, needing the silence and the sounds and smells of the lake to get some writing done. I slept the way you sleep only at camp, hard and deep, never moving an inch. And I started the day talking to my boys—Mac's sweet voice on the phone sounding a million miles away instead of an hour.

I drove into town for coffee and a croissant, and now I'm back to camp, in an Adirondack chair overlooking the peninsula. A group is gathered at the fire pit down the hill; I can't make out the words, but I hear the lilts and rises of a woman's voice from time to time. The clouds are low but not dark, and the green is impossibly vivid, everywhere you look.

If this journey has been the peeling of an onion, layer by layer, or the un-nesting of Russian dolls, shedding external selves like skin, it seems we are reaching the center.

The center is reached, once again, through silence, time, honesty, loss; by leaving behind all the voices and expectations, all the selves and costumes of other times, things that worked then but don't work any longer.

This is, I realize, middle age. But here's the thing: every new season of life is an invitation to leave behind the things of the season before, the trappings and traps that have long expired, right for then, no longer right for now.

Whatever passage you're facing—entering your twenties or your sixties, facing life alone for the first time in a long time or learning the new dance of partnership, becoming a parent or becoming an empty nester, leaving student life behind or becoming a student once again—has the potential to be your sea-change, your invitation to leave behind what's not essential and travel deeply into the heart of things. This is a pattern we can recreate all our lives, over and over, because who's ever totally finished leaving things behind?

One new thing that began to emerge: as I stopped ignoring my exhaustion and burying some of the brokennesses in my relationships, I started to have opinions. I mean, OPINIONS. I've always had opinions, certainly. But I've always been surrounded by people with strong opinions, too. And I've learned a very complicated geometry about which things I'm "allowed" to feel strongly about. There were so many things I left to other people to feel strongly about, so much so that I often bent under the weight of so many other peoples' strongly held opinions, tired from having to bridge all the gaps around me.

Truth-telling, though, is both contagious and addictive, and once you start doing it, it's hard to stop. All of a sudden, opinions fell out of my mouth left and right. I knew so well, so deeply that the areas in which my life went off course were the same areas in which I had abdicated responsibility and voice. I did what "people" thought would be good for me. I did what "should" have been done. I became what I was "expected" to become. And it did not get me where I wanted to be.

And so I'm learning to trust my feelings and my strong opinions, believing that they will be better guides than the nameless, faceless "they" I allowed to guide me for so long.

Many years ago, at breakfast with a mentor, I articulated, as best I could at that time, my greatest dream for my life. She was a great question-asker, and she kept pushing me for greater and greater specificity. And then what? What would that look like? Exactly how?

This is what I told her: I want to marry someone who feels like a partner, a true peer. I want to have little boys, and live in a house with a blue room where I write, and when I look out the window in the backyard, my boys will be playing soccer. When I'm done writing, I'll go down to the kitchen to stir something on the stove—a huge pot of red sauce, maybe, for the people who will gather around our table later—and while I stir, I'll talk on the phone with one of the pastors at our church. I wouldn't be working there, but I'd help in some way. I told her I wanted to write and be married and be a mom of boys and gather people in our home and help our church. Those are the things I wanted more than anything in the world.

I didn't move forward on this plan at all. I kept working at our church and then another, in an obsessive, workaholic way, letting work shadow over absolutely everything. Then I did become a writer, but the writing life quickly became the traveling-and-speaking life, almost accidentally—the obvious next step to everyone but me.

On paper, it looked like I was living that very dream from that conversation all those years ago. Unless the paper was my travel schedule. I wasn't standing at my stove very often, or hosting people around our table. I wasn't in town long enough to make a meaningful contribution at my church. I wasn't even a writer very often. I was grinding out a grueling travel schedule that I didn't enjoy but didn't know how to dismantle. Everyone was so happy about it, about each new opportunity. I didn't know till much later how profoundly unhappy I was about it. I longed to be back in that blue room, back at the stove, back on the lawn playing soccer with my boys.

And somewhere along the line, I developed the theology that said, "If it's working, it must be God's will; and if it's God's will, even if you hate it, you have to do it." I know, I know, you can see the errors in that a mile away, but that's how our weird little ideas are, so obvious to someone else but impossible to detangle ourselves.

I saw myself as a ball of energy, a firework, a high-capacity person, fearless and up for anything. But as I became more honest with myself, I didn't want the lifestyle being offered to me. I didn't like who I had to become in order to live in that world. And I didn't feel those good, whole, lovely feelings that people told me I was supposed to feel after doing a good job.

One thing I learned (which seems massively obvious in hindsight): we don't all love the same things.

Look at your deepest dreams, and who you've always been—the things you love even though no one else does, the times in your life when you feel the most beautiful, even if no one else thinks so.

And I found myself drawn more and more back to the water, to simplicity, to the margins and the mystery, to the ideas that don't fit on Twitter and a sense of nuance that doesn't fly on Facebook.

I found myself drawn to the table, old friends, quiet evenings, books. To home and family, life spent on porches, free of makeup and microphones. I found my way back to the girl I was in high school, in college: a hippie-ish bookworm who loved the simplicity of having everything she needed in a backpack.

There's something, I'm sure, about going back to the places you used to go to find the self you used to be. Maybe my long-ago essential self is more readily apparent here on these docks and benches and flaking chairs because so much of my life was spent here. Maybe that's why life at the lake continues to move me so deeply, because it draws me back to my past, who I've always been, underneath the recent shell I've been wearing—achievement, efficiency, productivity.

Heart and Yes

I remember the buzz of the needle from my first and second tattoos—that metallic rattle, high-pitched. It makes the muscles in my neck twitch, remembering the nagging pain that goes with the buzzing sound. I got my first tattoo during my senior year of high school on Casimir Pulaski day, a school holiday in Chicago thanks to the large Polish community. I told my parents I was going to do it, but they weren't too worried. I'd been fainting at the sight of a needle all my life—in doctors' offices, at the mall getting my ears pierced. When I came home and showed my mom the small Chinese symbol under the bandage, my mom said, "Bill, you're not going to believe this . . ."

Two years later, in Santa Barbara, a red-headed man named Sebastian put a small vine on my toe, and a tiny butterfly on my best friend Annette's toe. We were nineteen then, and now nineteen years later, here I am again, that buzzing sound ringing in my ears, offering up the tender pale flesh of my forearms, a heart on one, the word *yes* in my friend Lindsay's elegant cursive on the other, navy and careful.

The heart—blood red, perfectly simple, just exactly the way a child would draw a heart—is about love, of course. It's about God's love, about the revolutionary and foreign idea that I am loved by God, no matter what. Every Christian learns that early on. But that wild love is a difficult one to experience, for many of us. For me. I understand conditions, proving, record-keeping, tallies of grievances and offenses. I don't know much about unconditional. I feel like I'm just beginning to taste it for the first time.

When I pray, I picture a red heart—that perfectly simple red heart—and in the silence, I am reminded of God's love, that it began before I was born, that it will continue far past the end of my life. Before the day begins—kids, coffee, toast, little socks, little shoes, deadlines and decisions—before all that, I close my eyes, and I picture that red heart, and I remind myself what is true: that God loves me, and that there's nothing I can do in this new day to earn more love—*nothing.* And also that there's nothing I can do in this new day to ruin or break that love—*nothing.* I can't imagine anything more life-changing for an earner like me. That love is secure no matter what, no matter what, no matter what. No matter what I do or don't do, no matter whether I succeed or fail, no matter if I perform well or fall apart.

When I begin the day drenched in that love—that centering awareness of my worth and connection to God—the day is different. I don't have to scramble or hustle. Fear dissipates, and what I'm left with is warmth, creativity, generosity. I can make and connect and create and tell the truth, because my worth isn't on the line every time, at every moment. Unconditional love changes everything. It *is* changing everything. I can rest. I can fail. I can admit need and weakness. I can exhale. It's changing everything.

And so, that red heart. I wanted to carry it with me, and I wanted it on my left arm. I'm left handed, and I want that love to be the fuel. Whatever I build from here on out, whatever I make, whatever I write, whatever I create, I want the fuel that propels it to be love—not competition, not fear, not proving.

And *yes*: the word sparked for me for the first time two summers ago, when I was right smack dab in the middle of the lost-rushed-push-push-push season, aching for a change I didn't yet have the words to articulate. I went on a retreat—that same retreat where I learned to throw candy once again.

As I sat at O'Hare, ready to depart, I texted a friend who'd been on the same retreat the summer before. What am I getting myself into? I asked. What do I need to know? My friend Chris, who I've known for many years, who has been a big brother and encourager for almost a decade, replied with this: "Say YES. Jump. Hog the coconut shrimp."

I didn't know what any of it meant, of course, but a few hours in, I relayed those three instructions to my new friends. We did indeed hog the coconut shrimp, and it was impossibly delicious. And then we found ourselves scrambling up a cliff, ready to jump. The men were jumping, and it seemed like maybe the women were going to hang back, appreciate the view. I started to turn back to where the rest of the women were. And then Bryson yelled after me, just as I was turning away, “Shauna! Hey, Shauna! I thought you said we say yes! I thought you told me we jump!”

And so I jumped. And so I said yes, and that word became a shorthand between us, a symbol for being awake, for being alive, for showing up, for jumping. We texted it across the country to one another: “Are you saying yes?” “I said yes today!” “Say yes, say yes, say yes.”

I bought a sweatshirt that said SAY YES in navy and gold, and I wore it constantly, like a lucky charm, like a best friend. A reminder of this sweet, wide-open way of living, wholehearted, connected, wholly there. Words that hadn’t described me for a long time, but words that I aspire to.

Saying yes means not hiding. It means being seen in all your imperfections and insecurities. Saying yes is doing scary things without a guarantee that they’ll go perfectly. Saying yes is telling the truth even when it’s weird or sad or impossibly messy. Saying yes is inviting chaos, and also possibility. Saying yes is building a new future, regardless of the past. Saying yes is jumping in anyway.

One part of this journey, of course, was learning to say no. I couldn’t have remade my life without that very important word. But it’s not the word that I want to be my knee-jerk response to all of life. My response to pressure and expectations: no. But the word I want to say to beauty and freedom and soulfulness and life and play and creativity and challenge and God's wild and expansive love? Yes, yes, yes. Always yes.

And so, those two: the red heart and the word *yes*, the heart on my writing hand, the invitation *yes* on the other. My friend Sarah and I drove to the city on a rainy Tuesday, having set aside the afternoon for more than a month, having talked about this day, literally, for years. In the middle of the night, sometimes, on vacation, we'd say, "Let's do it right now!" But we never did, and we always meant to, and then I had a moment, a need to mark this new passage through to a new way of living, and I told her, "I'm going this month. You in?"

She was, and we were nervous right when we arrived, jittery, giggly. We talked to each other to take our minds off the needle, chatting about anything we could think of to cut through its noise. We planned a dinner party, talked through the menu and the table settings. We talked about kids and school and capsule wardrobes, and I'm sure all the men, all the tattoo artists, were rolling their eyes at these two moms, chatting the day away, giggly and euphoric.

Our old friend Ryan owns the shop, so I'd met most of the artists at Ryan and Emily's wedding last year. I had officiated, and my brother was the best man, and the ceremony was on the rooftop of a glassblowing factory on a gorgeous windy spring night.

And then exactly a year later, Sarah and I took turns talking each other through the nagging pain. After it was done, we walked around the corner to Eleven City Diner, too excited to go straight home. She had a mimosa and French toast, and I had an extra spicy Bloody Mary and a club sandwich, and we sat so happily on that foggy cool day, in the warm diner, high-ceilinged and classic.

I know some people think tattoos are insane or tacky or passé. But for me, these are the lines I've drawn in the sand—the daily, visual, tactile, with-me-all-the-time twin symbols for how I want to live, with great love and openness. These are the symbols of my future, of my calling, of my identity. I'm loved, and I choose to say yes. Yes. Yes.

Ballard Locks

Aaron and I are firecrackers, both of us—deep-feeling, mercurial, creative, passionate. We want what we want; we dream hard.

We fell hard, romance and wildness, going to plays and rock shows, talking all night, slow-dancing and running around the city. We met the week I turned twenty-two.

I was a writer, a feminist, prickly about all things church-and-faith related. I was fresh from four years in California, back home and testing the waters of a world I thought I'd never return to. I had my dukes up all the time: I'm not who you think I am. I'm not only a pastor's daughter. Please see me for more than that. Please see a poet and a fighter and a thinker. Please see me.

I'd made a mess of things in Santa Barbara, in some ways. In some ways, I'd made something beautiful—a person, a whole self, a messy collage of a million books and a thousand walks on the beach and a hundred late nights and a half-dozen heartbreaks. But when I got to the end of that wild season, I wanted to reconnect all the various pieces of my life to the spiritual part of my life. And looking back, I didn't know how to do that anywhere but home.

I went to work at the church my parents started. And on the first day of that new job, I met Aaron. I'd actually met him one time before—I watched his band play once when I was back for a Christmas break during college.

We were talking about that moment just recently. We were twenty, maybe.

What would we have thought if someone had whispered to us, "That's the person who will affect your life more than any other individual, forever. Your child will have her eyes, his voice"? How can it be that all those years ago something inside each of us sought out the other, believed so deeply in what the other might bring to our life? And how can it be that it is true?

Aaron told me he thought I was pretty for the first time while we kayaked together at a camp in Lake Geneva. I made it awkward, of course, disagreeing with him, telling him that it was a nice thing to say, but it wasn't true, obviously, empirically. Poor dude. Twenty-two years old, trying to talk to a girl he works with, and now she's unloading everything she learned in Women's Studies and every tender part of her heart, all wrapped up in theories and feminism. It took me about a decade and a half to just learn to say thank you. Full disclosure: I'm still working on that one.

He was a worship leader, and while I'd established pretty

firmly in college that I had a thing for musicians, I did not have a thing for worship leaders. Please. I barely had a thing for worship at that point, and I read onto him all the stereotypes—he's uncomplicated, happy-clappy all the time. No depth, no darkness, no beautiful weird complexity, no questions.

I can barely even type that now. It is with great affection that I tell you Aaron is the weirdest, deepest, wildest-minded, wildest-hearted person I know. He's all questions, a galaxy of what-if and why-not and could-it-be. Everything I thought about this sweet, uncomplicated, long-haired worship leader was a thousand-percent wrong. And I fell hard.

I thank God for that long-haired worship leader I got so wrong all those years ago. I thank God for every ounce of his dreaming, boundary-breaking, future-oriented mind and heart. I thank God for the grace he gives me time after time. I thank God for a partner who makes intentional space for who I am, even when I don't always make it for myself.

I tell people all the time that I'd never be a writer without Aaron, and it's true. I believe in being sensible and safe. I hate criticism, and people writing things about me online—especially about how I look—undoes me.

We've built a life and a family on love and art and messiness, and fifteen years later we're still trusting that there's plenty of space in this life we've created for two dreams, two passionate wild-hearted makers.

For many years, we traveled so much for work, together and separately, that our wedding anniversary became little more than a blip—we'd add on a day to the work trip, or get a sitter and have a quick dinner out.

And then four years ago, Aaron surprised me and took me to New York for two nights; and it was so rich and so needed and such a space of love and reconnection that we reset our attitude toward our anniversaries—we plan out months ahead of time where we want to go and what we want to do.

This year we went to Seattle. Earlier that month, we learned that two friends of ours—both married, both with children—had had an affair. We were absolutely, totally shocked.

It plunged us into a very deep set of questions about marriage and secrecy and friendship, and what it looks like to build durable, whole, healthy marriages.

Aaron and I talked about it a lot, it seemed, trying to make sense of it. If this happened to them, what would stop it from happening to us? What makes a good marriage? How do you know?

On the last afternoon of our anniversary trip to Seattle, we took a long walk through Ballard. We walked from one end of the neighborhood to the other, and we ended up winding across the locks on narrow metal bridges, all the way across, all the way back.

And as we walked, Aaron and I talked about our marriage in a way we never had. We'd realized, from watching our friends, that affairs don't come out of nowhere, but that often they find a place to wedge themselves when there's an expanse of distance in a marriage, when there's a vulnerability. So we talked about our marriage, over the years, and our vulnerabilities.

We talked about what had happened to create our most fragile seasons, and what repaired them. We talked about the kinds of people and personalities and attention that we might find ourselves vulnerable to, if we weren't careful. We apologized to one another for the things we did, over the years, to allow distance to stretch; and we talked about what shores up that distance, what ways of living and interacting help us connect in deep ways, keep the vulnerabilities from growing too great.

I never imagined that you could talk about those things in a marriage. I almost can't believe we did, as we inched our way over the locks, water rushing under our feet, low, gray sky above us.

The trip was romantic and silly and sweet—we rode a Ferris wheel and held hands. We slept in and had a great dinner with friends. But that conversation on the locks: that's the heart of marriage. That was the stuff, I think, that we're usually afraid to say out loud but loses its power once you share it. We talked about what we're afraid of, what we want for our lives, together and separately, who we fear we could become if we're not careful.

So there was wine and romance and a fancy hotel, but what mattered most was a cold, gray walk across the locks, saying the things you never say, taking the power out of them, and making us stronger.

New Fuel

I'm walking the last steps of this journey—not the life-living of it, but the story-telling. I spoke with one of my editors on the phone recently—I was standing on our front porch, kicking dead leaves with my bare feet; she was in North Carolina, and I imagined her in her office, book-lined and cozy. (I've never been in it, but I'm hoping it's both book-lined and cozy.) I told her that I was having a hard time finishing the book, like every author has said to every editor since the beginning of time. But this time it felt different to me.

Every previous run-up to publication involved mounting anxiety, jittery fearful energy that propelled me into a bout of manic work and equally manic worrying. I'd tie myself up in knots, produce pages and pages when only a new paragraph was required, try a new recipe five times in a row, into the middle of the night. I've always asked for help in a panicky email to friends, put myself on lockdown, canceled plans.

This time is different, though: the struggle is not managing the anxiety and the fear. I'm struggling instead to drum up the necessary energy to finish, because I've always been fueled by fear and anxiety. Once you stop using those fuels to power your life, it's like jumping off a cigarette boat onto a sailboat: disorientingly quiet, steady, calm. I love the calm. I've been aching for it for years. I love the peace and connectedness I've discovered along this journey . . . but those terrifying spikes of panic sure did help me get books finished.

I told her that this journey from pushing to peace had changed my life . . . and that one of the unexpected complexities is that I didn't need what I used to need from my work. I had learned the hard way what achievement could and couldn't give, and my newfound learning made me want to cook dinners and snuggle with my boys and read novels, and not really care so much about what anyone "out there" thought about it. This is freedom, but is this the end of the road for a writer?

I find myself confused about the career I've found myself in: if the white-hot fire to be heard, to say something, to put something beautiful and honest out into the vast silence isn't fanned by fear or desire to be respected or need to be seen, then what's left? Do I have anything left to say? Or should I close my laptop and stop this endless chattering, this endless need to say something, anything?

Another way to say it: what powers our work when it's no longer about addiction to achievement?

The last pages of this book have gone unwritten for a slightly unnerving amount of time. It's winter, and I find myself utterly not interested in finishing. I'm reading voraciously, making tacos and curries, folding laundry, taking walks. I'm going to bed early with thick novels, watching old movies with the boys, setting the table for cozy meals with friends, making menus filled with winter flavors: steak, potatoes, rosemary, garlic, red wine.

The stack of pages sits on my dresser, red pen resting on top. The documents on my computer go untouched for days on end. Frankly, this isn't like me. I am a procrastinator, and (like most writers, I think) I write in fits and starts. But there's a new thing happening in me right now—a detachment, almost.

Writing has always been a struggle for me—I love it; I avoid it; I fear I'll never make my deadline. Most writers I know are a touch neurotic about it. I always have been. And writing has been so deeply tied to my identity—so many of my friends are writers and English majors, bookworms, word nerds. This is what we do. The craft, the smell of old books, and on and on.

A few nights ago, a friend joined us for dinner and his daughter came, too—a senior English major, working on a thesis about Flannery O'Connor. Oh, I loved talking with her about narrative and theme. I wrote my senior thesis on Edith Wharton and Henry James, and when you ask for a book recommendation from me, hold on: I'm going to give you at least a dozen, or fifty.

My love affair with books endures, or, if anything, is growing. My appreciation for a well-crafted sentence or a perfectly chosen word is only rising, and my fascination with narrative and characterization and revelation, especially in memoir, is akin to an obsession.

My love for reading remains, but my desire to write is conspicuously waning . . . and I wonder sometimes if it's because writing has become—or maybe always was—a way of proving myself, defining myself, articulating something about my identity and worth.

Of course it is: who writes four books in a decade without having a little something to prove? I wasn't the smart one in my English program. I know that no one put money on me being the writer among us. I was a pastor's daughter who married a charming worship leader and worked for another well-known pastor: for the first decade of my professional life, I spoke on behalf of those three articulate, passionate, smart men. I became an expert in crafting and supporting their voices, and I wondered, deep down, in a tiny, secret place, if there was room for my voice. I was fairly sure there wasn't.

Late one night, a couple of years ago, a group was gathered around a fireplace and one friend asked this question: "What do you wish you could go back and tell your self from ten years ago?"

I said, "I'd tell her I know you can't even imagine it now, but you don't have to only speak the words of your father, your husband, your pastor. Your work doesn't have to be simply facilitating their work. You have your own voice. And you can use it."

I don't know if I would have even believed that message ten years ago. But here we are—it has been a profound honor to find and use that voice. I'm thankful every day to be a writer, to work with words and ideas and sentences, to get to tell the truth about the world as I see it.

But what used to be a highly charged need to scrawl out my deepest, most honest, most intense and freighted truths has become something else. I don't need the same things I've needed from it, along the way.

So if it isn't about those things, why do it? If I wake up in the morning, and live each day with a deep, soul-altering awareness that I am loved just as I am, and that love is the only true currency, then the laptop starts to gather dust, and it's terribly easy to curl up with an old novel, all drenched in grace and contentedness.

Why do it? Because writing has become my love letter, my way of telling the love story that's changed my life.

What fuels me now is love. It's slower and deeper, less combustible and exciting. But it burns within my heart with such warmth and crackle that I never want to go back to the old fuel. The words come more slowly now, and the process is less frantic and jittery, and I think that's just fine.

And the Soul Felt Its Worth

O holy night!
The stars are brightly shining
It is the night of the dear Savior's birth!
Long lay the world in sin and error pining
Till he appear'd and the soul felt its worth.
A thrill of hope the weary soul rejoices
For yonder breaks a new and glorious morn!

I think it's taken me almost forty years to actually feel the worth of my soul. All of a sudden, the words from that carol I've sung a thousand times stop me in my tracks. *He appears, and the soul feels its worth.* Jesus is born, love comes down from heaven in human form, and the soul feels its worth.

Because that's what I've been searching for, wringing myself out for, zigzagging the country for: a sense of my own worth. That's what we're craving: the sense that we matter, that someone sees us, that we are loved and valued. And so some of us try to earn it. Some of us try to avoid the pain of unworthiness by escaping, with drugs or shopping or sex or whatever. Some of us pretend to be perfect, instead of admitting that behind the image, we feel as small and unworthy as we ever have.

The soul's worth, though, doesn't come from earning or proving. Image doesn't matter. Outrunning the emptiness doesn't work for long. Each soul, every soul is worthy, because God made every soul, and because of his love, his Son came to earth and walked among us, because God's love for us is so deep and wide and elaborate that he wants to be with us, to walk with us, to teach us how to live in that love and worthiness.

It is only when you understand God's truly unconditional love that you begin to understand the worth of your own soul—not because of anything you've done, but because every soul is worthy, every one of us is worthy of love, having been created by and in the image of the God of love.

It was there all along, that thing I've been aching for, that deep sense of worthiness and love. It was there all along, for all of us. For so many of us, what religion taught us was how to feel ashamed. For many years, my spiritual life was one more place to measure up and be found wanting.

This awareness of love, though, this sense of the soul's worth, not because of my own doing but because of God's great love—this changes everything. For the first time in my life, my faith is the softest part of my life, the most healing, most life-giving space in my heart. Instead of one more thing to do or try or fail at, my relationship with God is the force of love that heals up all the other bruised and broken parts. Prayer is the safest, most nurturing activity I practice, almost like sitting in the sun, face tilted up, or imagining yourself as a child, crawling up into the lap of a treasured, trusted grandparent.

I can hardly believe my fingers as I type this. I left behind all the lovey-dovey Jesus-is-my-boyfriend business years ago. I had signed on to be a soldier, tough and faithful, bandaging my own wounds, not running to God for every little bump or bruise. But acting tough for too long makes the soft tissue of your heart start to toughen as well. It severs your relationship to your soul, little by little, till you find yourself doubting the importance of something as woo-woo as a soul in the first place.

In three of the four Gospels, Jesus asks, "What good is it for someone to gain the whole world, yet forfeit their soul?" This is another one of those verses that I've read so many times over the years but has gained so much new meaning and weight in this season. "The whole world" is essentially all the things you've ever wanted—whatever success means to you, or the good life, or what it looks like to live the dream. Many of us have been living the life we've always wanted, or so it seems. But just under the surface of that lovely life is exhaustion, or isolation, or emptiness. It doesn't matter how pretty things look on the outside if on the inside, there's an ache from a lifetime of trying to prove your worth.

Many of us, myself included, considered our souls necessary collateral damage to get done the things we felt we simply had to get done—because of other peoples' expectations, because we want to be known as highly capable, because we're trying to outrun an inner emptiness. And for a while we don't even realize the compromise we've made. We're on autopilot, chugging through the day on fear and caffeine, checking things off the list, falling into bed without even a real thought or feeling or connection all day long, just a sense of having made it through. We begin to think the soul is expendable—a luxury, maybe, something optional but certainly not required.

But then someone starts talking about your soul—maybe at church, maybe in a book. Someone starts talking about things like grace and rest and peace, and the soul feeling its worth, and that language feels so foreign and so beautiful, like water in a desert, like one bright bud pushing up in an otherwise arid landscape. And like a song you used to love but haven't heard for years, something breaks through: that's what I've been missing. That's it. My soul.

Our souls are of fundamental importance, truly the only things besides our physical bodies that we are entirely, independently responsible to steward. Many of us take care of our bodies with great attentiveness, conscious to fill our bodies with good things, to rest them well, to move and breathe deeply. After years of being careless with both my body and soul, trusting in some vague way that they'd probably be fine no matter what, I'm learning that both body and soul require more tenderness and attentiveness than I had imagined.

Our souls are what allow us to connect—with God, with other people, with nature, with art. Without a soul, you can walk and drive and sleep, but you can't love, you can't weep, you can't feel. You can't make great art—or at least not for long.

A soul is not required for a robot. Or for a machine. Or for a set of ideas or theories. But a soul is profoundly necessary for a human. It's from our souls that we love, that we feel, that we create, that we connect.

And so Jesus' question—*what does is profit someone to gain the whole world and lose their soul?*—is a way of demonstrating the paradox of getting everything you want, only to find yourself unable to truly experience those things you've worked so hard for. All those things you wanted out there? The world, as it were? Art and food and connection and beauty and experiences and meaning? You cannot feel or taste or touch those things without a soul. And so what good are they to you, if you gain them at the expense of the softest, most precious part of you?

What kills a soul? Exhaustion, secret keeping, image management.

And what brings a soul back from the dead? Honesty, connection, grace.

Whatever you've achieved, wherever you've arrived—a dollar amount in the bank, a number on the scale, that award or promotion or perfect house—whatever it is, if in order to get there, you laid your soul down, believing it was unnecessary baggage, or an acceptable sacrifice, I'm here to tell you, with great love and tenderness, that you're wrong; and that I'd love to take you by the hand, and walk back as far as we need to, down the road of your past, to find it, like a sweater you dropped walking to class, like a scarf that slipped off your shoulders unnoticed.

Bring in the Love

Are you tired? Worn out? Burned out on religion? Come to me. Get away with me and you'll recover your life. I'll show you how to take a real rest. Walk with me and work with me—watch how I do it. Learn the unforced rhythms of grace. I won't lay anything heavy or ill-fitting on you. Keep company with me and you'll learn to live freely and lightly.

—Matthew 11:28–30, *The Message*

It is achingly, bone-rattlingly cold in Chicago, but cloudless and blue-skied, crisp to the point of shattering, icy sidewalks and furnaces kicking on around the clock with labored thunks.

Today I was craving garlic and tomatoes, so in between the scribbling of sentences, I melted several cloves of garlic and a couple handfuls of halved grape tomatoes into oil over low heat on the stove. The sharp garlic smell filled the house and then began to mellow, as the tomatoes slipped out of their skins, blistered, softened. A steaming bowl of those melted, fragrant tomatoes and garlic were just the thing for the starkness of the day, the severe chill.

My task for the day: to find the words to leave you with, to wrap my mind and heart and letters and words around the last three and whatever years, and tell you something about it all.

This is what I want to tell you: it's better here, here in the place of love. This journey has brought about a meaningful transformation in every single part of my life. Every single part. My prayer life, my marriage, my family life, my friendships. I enjoy my work more. I feel a deep well of gratitude, a clean and grateful desire to live a life of meaning. I have the energy to live well, to dedicate myself to the things that matter to me, and that God has called me to. I have the security to truly rest, to truly enjoy this extraordinary world and all its offerings—books and art and meals and people and conversations and cities and beaches and night skies. And while I am deeply appreciative of the charms of this glittering world, I feel a sense of patience where I used to feel slight anxiety about the beauty of it: will I see it all? What if I miss something?

In the space that used to be filled with a whirring ball of anxiety, now there is a new patience, a new settledness, a new desire to be just exactly where I am right now. I'm reveling in this new patience, this new groundedness, this new sense of peace. It's so foreign, and it's so lovely.

The deep well of contentedness that I feel these days is nothing short of a miracle, and it's one I am thankful for every single day.

For a while, I placed my marriage, my family, and my soul on the altar of productivity, of hustle, of competency and efficiency. I can't adequately express the regret I feel for having done that, or the gratitude I feel for pulling them back down off the altar before it was too late.

I don't know what would have happened if I'd continued down that road another year. Or two. Or ten.

A couple of days ago we had lunch with two rabbis, married to one another. I'd met the husband, but this was my first time meeting his wife. They were smart and funny and passionate, and we thoroughly enjoyed our time with them.

At a certain point, we talked about work and life and time and parenting. I told them a little bit about the changes I'd been making—slower, less task-oriented, less driven. The husband, perceptively, turned to Aaron, and asked about what this meant for him, for the shared responsibilities of our life. We all laughed, but it was a serious and valid question.

Aaron said, "Yeah, things are messier. She's not running around cleaning and fussing all the time. I have to do more, and I'm not great at that stuff, and there's more that we just leave undone. But here's the thing: I have my wife back. And it's totally, completely worth it."

That's why this journey matters. Because I was on a dangerous track, where I was giving the best of myself to people and things "out there," while the tender inner core of my life and my home were increasingly stretched, pressurized, brittle. And now they're not. Now the most beautiful, well-tended, truly nurtured and nourished parts of my life are the innermost ones, not the flashy public ones. That's just as it should be.

We are, as I've mentioned, not a family of conventional traditions. There are a couple rituals, though, that we've developed over the years that I truly love. The first: Christmas and New Year's on the beach. The week before Christmas we open presents, celebrate with various family and friends. We're a part of the many Christmas services at our church, and we watch our kids in their holiday programs—this year Mac was the innkeeper, and Henry sang "Rockin' Around the Christmas Tree" with the rest of his third-grade class—with extremely festive motions. And then early on Christmas morning, we throw our bags in the car and meet the rest of my family at the airport for the flight south just as the sun is coming up.

And on that trip, there are two more traditions: on New Year's Eve, we batter and deep-fry everything in sight—this year, lobster, conch, potatoes, pickles, bananas, baby bell peppers stuffed with cheese. And then after dinner and before the countdown to midnight, we sit in a circle and take turns reading lists we've made of the ten greatest blessings of the year.

And this year, our son Henry—perceptive, articulate, old-souled—told this circle of friends and family that one of the things he was most thankful for was that his parents don't work too much to spend time with him. Tears, of course, sprang to my eyes. We don't talk with him about this stuff, necessarily. We just do it and trust that he notices. And he does.

He talked about several other things he's thankful for—his grandparents, his favorite teacher Miss Gillespie, our basketball hoop, and then his tenth blessing was the word *connected*. He said, "You know, I just feel like my mom and dad and Mac and I are really connected."

Maybe you've always managed your time and your anxieties and your compulsions just perfectly. Maybe your kids have always felt super-duper connected. Maybe your marriage has always been a model of intimacy.

But that's not my story. I was heading for a crash, having lost touch with my essential self and the hand of God to guide me. I cannot express to you how easily that connection we now experience could have been compromised forever in my panicky need to outrun my fear and hustle for my identity.

My life is smaller, slower, simpler. My days are less complicated. I sleep better and wake with a heart of deep gratefulness. I've become able to appreciate silliness again, and subtle beauty, instead of the volume of my life being so screechingly loud only fireworks could get my attention.

I feel prouder of my smaller, simpler, quieter, more connected life than I ever did when all of life was screaming along. I thought I would feel a deep gladness if I broke my back for my work. I broke my back for my work, and all I felt was back-breaking pain. That rush of love never did come, until now. Until I realized that the love I was looking for all along is never found in the hustle. You can't prove it or earn it or compete for it. You can just make space for it, listen for it, travel all the way down to the depth of your soul, into the rhythmic beating of your very own heart, where the very spirit of God has made his home, and that's where you'll find it.

You'll find it in the faces of the people who've known you all your life, who sit around your table every week, the children whose noses you kiss while they're sleeping. You'll find it in prayer, when you sit in silence sensing the presence of Christ resurrected.

Mac, our four-year-old, is the snuggliest, most affectionate little person on earth. And when he wants a hug or a kiss, he'll fling out his arms and bellow, "Bring in the love!" in a deep voice, like a radio deejay. And then when you scoop him up, he pats you over and over on the back with his little hands and says, "There it is. There's the love. There's the love."

Here it is. Here's the love. Here's the love: it's in marriage and parenting. It's in family and friends. It's in sacrifice and forgiveness. It's in dinner around the coffee table and long walks. It's in the hands and faces of the people we see every day, in the whispers of our prayers and hymns and songs. It's in our neighborhoods and churches, our classrooms and living rooms, on the water and in the stories we tell.

And let me tell you where it's not: it's not in numbers—numbers in bank accounts, numbers on scales, numbers on report cards or credit scores. The love you're looking for is never something you can calculate. It's not something you can buy or earn or hustle for.

It's something you discover in the silence, in the groundedness, in the sacred risky act of being exactly who you are—nothing more, nothing less. In that still, holy space, the love you've been frantically hunting for all along will bloom within your ribs. And you will know, in that moment, that it has been there all along, like a whisper, the very Spirit of God himself.

The bad news is that there is no finish line here, no magical before-and-after. Probably you will not always live in this new, brave, grounded space. Let me be clear with you: I don't. I still get pushed off center, thrown into fear and proving, wound up into a tangled mess of expectations and opinions of who I should be and what I should do.

But there's good news, too: if we just keep coming back to the silence, if we keep grounding ourselves, as often as we need to, in God's wild love, if we keep showing up and choosing to be present in both the mess and in the delight, we will find our way home, even if the road is winding, and full of fits and starts.

We will find our way home.

The Journey

By Mary Oliver

One day you finally knew
what you had to do, and began,
though the voices around you
kept shouting
their bad advice—
though the whole house
began to tremble
and you felt the old tug
at your ankles.
"Mend my life!"
each voice cried.
But you didn't stop.
You knew what you had to do,
though the wind pried
with its stiff fingers
at the very foundations,
though their melancholy
was terrible.
It was already late
enough, and a wild night,

and the road full of fallen
branches and stones.
But little by little,
as you left their voices behind,
the stars began to burn
through the sheets of clouds,
and there was a new voice
which you slowly
recognized as your own,
that kept you company
as you strode deeper and deeper
into the world,
determined to do
the only thing you could do—
determined to save
the only life you could save.

Acknowledgments

So much love to the Hybels and Niequist families, especially Nana Lynne and Papa Bill, Uncle Todd, and Nana D and Papa D.

Thanks to Melody Martinez, Amanda Hybels, Matt and Casey Sundstedt, Blaine and Margaret Hogan, Brannon Anderson, Rachel Reiman, Matt and Kristi Lundgren, Paul Johnson and Rhianna Godfrey, Brian and Jorie Johnson, and Steve and Sarah Carter—the local, daily pals who make our life rich and meaningful.

Love and thanks to Annette and Andrew Richards, Emily and Ryan Gardner, Monica Robertson, Kirsten Davidson, Jen Hatmaker, Glennon Melton, and Brené Brown—dear friends who, despite distance, teach me so much.

So much love to the Willow family and the Practice tribe—you guide and inspire me.

Special thanks to Dr. Bob Watson and Mary McKeon for walking me home—toward Christ, toward wholeness, toward better ways of living.

Love to the Lodge Family, especially Bob and Maria Goff, Don and Betsy Miller, Bryson and Emily Vogeltanz,

Cameron Strang, Nichole Nordeman, and Brian and MacKenzie Canlis: you all gave me the courage to change my life in ways I desperately needed.

Much gratitude to Carolyn McCready, Lauren Winner, and Angela Scheff—I'm the luckiest writer on earth to work with three brilliant, loving women like you. You went above and beyond on this one. You three are spectacular, and I'm endlessly thankful.

Thanks as well to Chris Ferebee, my agent and my friend, and to Tim Schraeder, Londa Alderink, Greg Clouse, Curt Diepenhorst, Jennifer VerHage, and the rest of the kind and capable HarperCollins Christian team.

And I'll end the way I began, with heart-bursting amounts of love for my three precious boys: Aaron, Henry, and Mac. I love you with my whole heart.

Cold Tangerines

Celebrating the Extraordinary Nature of Everyday Life

Shauna Niequist

Cold Tangerines — now available in softcover — is a collection of stories that celebrate the extraordinary moments hidden in your everyday life. It is about God, and about life, and about the thousands of daily ways in which an awareness of God changes and infuses everything. It is about spiritual life, and about all the things that are called nonspiritual life that might be spiritual after all. It is the snapshots of a young woman making peace with herself and trying to craft a life that captures the energy and exuberance we all long for in the midst of the fear and regret and envy we all carry with us. It is both a voice of challenge and song of comfort, calling you upward to the best possible life and giving you room to breathe, to rest, to break down and break through.

Cold Tangerines offers bright and varied glimpses of hope and redemption, in and among the heartbreak and boredom and broken glass.

Bittersweet

Thoughts on Change, Grace, and Learning the Hard Way

Shauna Niequist

"The idea of *bittersweet* is changing the way I live, unraveling and re-weaving the way I understand life. Bittersweet is the idea that in all things there is both something broken and something beautiful, that there is a sliver of lightness on even the darkest of nights, a shadow of hope in every heartbreak, and that rejoicing is no less rich even when it contains a splinter of sadness.

"Bittersweet is the practice of believing that we really do need both the bitter and the sweet, and that a life of nothing but sweetness rots both your teeth and your soul. Bitter is what makes us strong, what forces us to push through, what helps us earn the lines on our faces and the calluses on our hands. Sweet is nice enough, but bittersweet is beautiful, nuanced, full of depth and complexity. Bittersweet is courageous, gutsy, earthy."

Shauna Niequist, a keen observer of life with a lyrical voice, writes with the characteristic warmth and honesty of a dear friend: always engaging, sometimes challenging, but always with a kind heart. You will find *Bittersweet* savory reading, indeed.

EL SEGUNDO PUBLIC LIBRARY
00534 7207